THE WORSHIPFUL COMPANY

MIA BALL

The Worshipful Company of Brewers

A SHORT HISTORY

HUTCHINSON BENHAM

LONDON

Hutchinson Benham Ltd
3 Fitzroy Square, London W1

An imprint of the Hutchinson Group

London Melbourne Sydney Auckland
Wellington Johannesburg and agencies
throughout the world

First published 1977
© Brewers' Company 1977

Set in Monotype Garamond

Printed in Great Britain by
The Anchor Press Ltd, and bound by
Wm Brendon & Son Ltd, both of
Tiptree, Essex

ISBN 0 09 127850 3

Contents

List of Illustrations

Colour Plates

Charter granted by Elizabeth I to the Brewers' Company in 1579
The Company pall
The gateway to Brewers' Hall, Addle Street
Silver from the Company's collection

Black and White

Foreword

In an age of change it is fashionable, and reasonable, that existing social, moral and commercial standards should be challenged to test their relevance and contribution to the new society. Reasonable if the motivation for change is improvement, but, sadly, it is often motivated by misunderstanding.

The City and its institutions are going through a period of challenge and so perhaps it is timely, in thinking of its future role, to ponder on the enormous contribution made to its development by the City Livery Companies over many centuries. Trade protection society, trade administrators, guardians of quality, preservers of craft skills and benefactors – the Brewers' Company can claim to have been all these things.

It is proud of its long history; it is also proud that in the latter part of the twentieth century it is one of the few Livery Companies which can still claim to have close associations with its trade. It sees its future role clearly, not only as a trustee of its charitable funds but also as the voice of the London brewers.

When we asked Mia Ball, who was then a member of the staff of the Brewers' Company, to research our history, we said that we would like a book written to record the progress of the Worshipful Company of Brewers and its association with the City. We think that she has produced an excellent blend of historical fact and human interest which will add to the rich background of information about London and the people who have contributed to its greatness.

MASTER 1975–6

Chapter One

From Fraternity to Gild

IN 1292, the twentieth year of the reign of Edward I, the following entry appeared in the City Letter Book:

Edward, etc. to the Warden and Aldermen of the City of London, etc. Whereas it has been shown to us by certain brewers, citizens of London, that they had been prejudiced as to their franchise in relation to their trade by our Sheriffs of London, and by those appointed by us to hear plaints in London, and we have already enjoined you to inquire into the matter; but you nevertheless showing favour to the Sheriffs and the others, have delayed inquiry, and the brewers continue to suffer at the hands of the Sheriffs; we, wishing to provide a remedy, do command you to summons the Sheriffs aforesaid before you, and after hearing the complaints of the brewers to do therein according to justice, and allow them to enjoy such liberties and customes as they ought, and such as their predecessors used to enjoy.[1]

In the history of the Worshipful Company of Brewers the entry has a particular significance. It is the earliest written evidence for the existence of a body of brewers who had joined together to protect themselves and their trade. This body was to evolve through the centuries to become the Wardens and Commonalty of the Mistery of Brewers of the City of London, fourteenth in order of precedence among the City's eighty-four Livery Companies.

There is no evidence for the date when this association of brewers first came into being, but, considering what is known of the foundation of the Livery Companies in London, it is probable that the Brewers were one of the earliest groups of traders to come together as an organized trade gild. A list of the gilds known to have been in existence in the twelfth century indicates that these were formed first among members of the oldest and most important trades, such as the Goldsmiths, Fishmongers, Weavers and Butchers.[2] The importance of ale in the diet of the medieval Englishman and the fact that the art of brewing had been long established in England are sufficient to suggest that the brewers would have been likely to be numbered among these major traders.

The brewing of ale from barley had been known in England even prior to the Roman invasions. Tacitus, writing of the customs of the natives when the Romans arrived, stated that, 'For drink they use the liquid distilled from barley or wheat, after fermentation had given it a certain resemblance to wine',[3] and Julius Caesar made an interesting comment on the national brew: 'The Britons have vines but use them only for arbours in their gardens. They drink a high and mighty liquor, different from that of any other nation, made of barley and water. This drink is not so subtle in its effects as wine, but it is warming, even more nourishing, and leaves enough space for the performance of many actions before the spirits are quite vanquished.'[4]

Beer and mead clearly had an equal popularity among the Anglo-Saxons, and the mead-hall, or beer-hall, seems to have been the social centre of the community before the full establishment of Christianity saw this function taken over by the Church. In the beer-hall drinking was taken seriously, often ceremoniously, and in the society it fostered – warriors and retainers under a leader – it was the forerunner of the baronial hall of the later Middle Ages. It seems also that it was the Anglo-Saxons who founded the first English 'pubs', early ale-houses set up at the roadside, usually at a cross-road to attract passing travellers. These houses were distinguished as ale-houses by a pole set outside, the ale-stake, and if the house sold wine as well as ale, an ivy wreath was hung from the pole – the first inn signs.

The early ale-houses, however, were small, and brewing was done on a domestic level. The first brewing to be carried out on a large scale was done in the monasteries, the establishment of which throughout the country followed the spread of Christianity. All monasteries had their own brew-houses, and as the monks also provided bed and board for travellers, so considerable

Thomas à Becket embarking for England. From the thirteenth-century
MS *Vie de St Thomas. Mansell Collection*

quantities of ale were required. Monastery ale was frequently
good, and being brewed in large quantities, several different
strengths of ale could be economically produced. The barrels
would be marked +, + +, + + +, to denote pale, mild or strong.
Drunkenness among the clergy and guests was quite common,
judging by the number of decrees issued against intemperance
in the early Middle Ages.

Once the church became the social centre of every town and
village, it also became a place for drinking. After services, local
traders might do business in the nave over mugs of ale. When
complaints of drunkenness and rowdy behaviour resulted in
such activities being forbidden within the church, the business,
and the drinking, took place first in the churchyard and then in
the church-house, a building customarily erected next to the

church for social purposes connected with it. The church-house became the centre for many activities, and often a bakery and a brew-house would be attached to it. The church-house was run by the churchwardens and it was they who were responsible for raising funds for the church. This was done by holding quarterly 'church-ales', social gatherings at which much ale was bought and consumed to raise the necessary money. These ales were very popular, and the principle was extended to raise funds for a variety of causes;[5] they remained as the regular method of making money in local churches until forbidden under Cromwell.

Even the increased quantities of wine which were brought to England following the Norman Conquest do not seem to have lessened the popularity of ale, and there is evidence that the French themselves appreciated it. Thomas à Becket was sent to France in 1158 to secure the hand of the French Princess Margaret, daughter of Louis VII, for Henry, eldest son of Henry II, and it is recorded that among the gifts he took for the French King were two wagons which 'bore nothing but beer, made by a decoction of water from strong corn, and carried in iron-hooped barrels, to be given to the French, who admire liquor of this sort, for it is certainly a wholesome drink, clear, of the colour of wine and of superior flavour'.[6]

The place of ale in the national life was recognized in the drawing up of the Magna Carta in 1215, when a clause was written in requiring a standard measure for ale, and in 1267 Henry III introduced the Assize of Bread and Ale, which fixed the prices of these commodities according to local prices of wheat and malt, the Assize to be announced by the civic authorities (i.e. the Sheriffs) in each town. The Assize in London in 1276 fixed the price at $\frac{3}{4}$d. per gallon, with 1d. per gallon for strong ale, and the following year a further attempt at controlling the sale of ale was made when the Assize also declared that 'no brewster henceforth sell except by true measure, viz. the gallon, the potel and the quart. And that they be marked with the seal of the Aldermen, and that the tun be of 150 gallons and sealed by the Aldermen.'[7]

The importance attached to the price and supply of ale is relative to its place in the basic diet of all Englishmen in the

Middle Ages. It is only in comparatively modern times that bread and water have been regarded as the necessities of life; for centuries it was bread and ale that were considered the staple foods. Water supplies, drawn largely from communal wells and open conduits, were frequently contaminated and drinking the water could result in serious illness and death. But water was purified in the process of brewing, and then the use of malt as an ingredient promoted the belief that ale was a wholesome and nourishing drink. Indeed, so vital to life was ale considered that an ordinance in the City Letter Book for 1382 decreed that 'in order to assist the poor, bakers shall make bread at a farthing the piece and brewers shall sell ale by a farthing measure (the Mayor and Aldermen deeming it equally necessary to the poor as in the case of bread)'.[8]

Producing such a vital drink, the brewers of medieval London must have been among the leading traders. They were certainly numerous, for the survey for the Poll Tax levied in 1380 records over 1,000 brew-houses in the City, making one to every twelve inhabitants. The sale of their ale may not have made them as wealthy as the Goldsmiths or Weavers, but the very quantity of the trade must have given a large number of the brewers at least a degree of affluence, and these men would have been ranked, in the twelfth and thirteenth centuries, among the new middle class of merchants which emerged as the natural result of increased trade and prosperity within the City as a whole. And it was from this middle class that the first craft gilds drew their members ('craft' being at that time a word denoting trade in a broader sense than it is used today). An indication of the wealth of the Brewers and their position in the City at this time is given in Stow's *Survey of London*. Describing the Cripplegate postern, Stow states that 'This gate was new builded by the Brewers of London, in the year 1244'.[9] It is not possible to verify this statement, and Stow's last *Survey* only appeared in 1603, but if he is correct, the fact also points to the existence of some association of brewers in the early thirteenth century.

The craft gilds grew from the natural and spontaneous association of men involved in the same craft who wished to improve and protect their own trade. Such gilds were to spring up in most of the country's larger towns, but the City of London, larger and more prosperous than any other, was the first centre to see the development of a considerable number of specialized gilds with members wealthy and prominent enough to win for themselves an important place in the City's organization and government.

In the early years, craft gilds faced opposition to their very existence from the then established hierarchy in the City. The City had its own systems of government – it had received its first charter from Henry 1 in 1132, when the citizens were given the right to elect their own Sheriffs (the officials responsible for the collection of crown revenues and enforcing justice). When the charter was confirmed by John, the City was also given the right to elect its own Mayor (the first was Henry fitz Ailwin, elected in 1193) and the government was in the hands of the Mayor and the Court of twenty-four Aldermen. Their rule was not always popular, particularly with the rising mercantile class, who were keen to have some say themselves in the government of the City.

The thirteenth century saw repeated attempts by the citizens to have a Mayor elected who would represent their interests against the power of the Aldermen, who would usually ensure that their own candidate was chosen for the office. It was largely due to the united efforts of the new gilds that in 1271 citizens of London were able for the first time successfully to oppose the Aldermen and force the election of one Walter Hervey as Mayor, a man whom the merchants chose to represent their interests. The success on this occasion was short-lived, as after his term of office the Aldermen were again in command, and Hervey was accused of underhand activities on behalf of his supporters during his time as Mayor, and all his ordinances were overruled. Among the things he was accused of was allowing the Brewers to sell ale below the price fixed at the Assize.

It was undoubtedly in an attempt to prevent the citizens coming together to oppose them that, after the mayoralty of Hervey, the Aldermen had the formation of trade associations banned, and the ban largely explains the close links of the early trade gilds with the Church, and why many gilds started as religious fraternities. George Unwin in his book *The Gilds and Companies of London* has explained the situation thus: 'Association

Simon the Cellarer – a sarcastic reference to the worship of the cask.
From a fourteenth-century misericord in the parish church of St Laurence
Ludlow. *Radio Times Hulton Picture Library*

always needed a sanction, and the less an association of craftsmen
could rely on the tacit sanction of the civic authorities, the more
it needed the shelter and the sanction of the Church, which was
rarely refused in some form or other.'[10]

The powerful position of the Church in the medieval social
and governmental order meant that she could offer some protection from secular attack and hence an immunity from the penalties that could be enforced on the trade gilds if they placed
themselves under her patronage. The convenience of this
arrangement can be gathered from the fines known to have been

imposed on some unlicensed (or adulterine) gilds.[11] The Pipe Rolls of 1180 mention eighteen gilds which were fined amounts varying from 45 marks to $\frac{1}{2}$ mark; among those mentioned by name are the Goldsmiths, Pepperers (i.e. Grocers), Clothworkers and Butchers. However, the existence of a religious fraternity whose members happened to be drawn largely from the same trade did not imply that the Church was merely providing a cover for illegal activities. Men and women of the same trade tended to gravitate towards the same area of the City, and would, therefore, naturally attend the same church. A fraternity would sometimes take their church's saint as their own patron saint; all were known by the name of their chosen patron, and their ordinances gave prominence to the religious and charitable purposes of the fraternity. Money was subscribed for the support of poor members and to provide a decent funeral for all brethren; it was a general requirement that everyone should attend the funeral of a fellow member. A fraternity usually held official meetings four or five times a year for business and to distribute alms, and it was usual, too, for an annual feast to be held.

In some cases the gradual development of such a fraternity into an acknowledged craft gild, the primary purpose of which was the promotion of trade interests, can be clearly seen, as with the Goldsmiths' Fraternity of St Dunstan and the Grocers' Fraternity of St Anthony. In general, however, the links between fraternity and gild cannot be definitely traced. Some craft gilds appeared without any evidence of an earlier religious association, and in other instances a craft gild and religious fraternity for members of the same trade seem to have existed side by side and independently of each other. It would seem that this was the case among the brewers.

The Calendar of Wills in the Court of Hustings for 1361 provides evidence that a Fraternity of Brewers was connected with the Church of All-Hallows near the Wall,[12] but there is nothing to suggest any connection at that time between it and the Brewers' Gild, the existence of which is established by the evidence of the City Letter Book. In the case of the Brewers, fraternity and gild continued their separate existence for a time, but the fraternity gradually merged with the gild, which took over its religious and charitable functions and maintained the link with All-Hallows Church.

It was natural that the first trade gilds to establish themselves openly were those of the major crafts, whose members were often wealthy and important men in the City's commercial life. These men were in a better position than small traders to resist the opposition of the Aldermen, for the City's prosperity depended largely on them. By the end of the thirteenth century the leading merchants were themselves being elected as Aldermen, an open acknowledgement of the importance of the gilds to which they belonged. By this time, too, the wealthy gilds had got further protection for themselves by obtaining royal charters, following the example of the Weavers, who were incorporated in the middle of the twelfth century. A charter meant that a gild could no longer be suppressed as illegal. The acquisition of royal charters by the major craft gilds must have signalled the end of effective opposition by the Court of Aldermen, and when in 1310 the Lord Mayor, Richer de Reffham, granted several gilds the right to regulate their trade within the City, he was supported by the Aldermen. It is, however, worth noting that the terms of these early charters all gave prominence to the religious and charitable aims of the association, rather than any economic intent, and most were incorporated under the name of a patron saint rather than that of their trade.

When the Brewers' Gild received its first charter it was known as the Gild of St Mary and St Thomas the Martyr, i.e. Thomas à Becket. Why St Thomas à Becket should have been chosen as the Brewers' patron is unknown. In his lifetime he had had close links with the City, his father being a leading merchant with a house in Cheapside, and Becket had indeed been a noted drinker in his youth, but his only direct connection with the trade would seem to be on the occasion of his French visit as narrated above. A popular story handed down in the Brewers' Company is that Becket was chosen as patron when, following his martyrdom in 1170, many pilgrims made their way to his shrine at Canterbury, and drank many gallons of ale on the long journey, thus earning the gratitude of the Brewers! And like many legends there is probably a grain of truth in it. Chaucer's Canterbury pilgrims made use of the inns *en route*; at their first

The earliest surviving writ (as opposed to charter) granted the City of London, issued by William the Conqueror in 1067. *Courtesy of the Corporation of London Record Office*

place of call, the Tabard Inn at Southwark, food and drink were plentifully supplied:

> *Greet chere made our Hoste us everichon,*
> *And to the soper sette us anon,*
> *And served us with vitaille at the beste.*
> *Strong was the wyn, and wel to drinke us leste.*[13]

and the following day one member of the party, the Miller, was quite drunk, a circumstance he put down to the excellent Southwark ale.

Whatever their official titles, in the early fourteenth century the gilds were beginning to function openly as declared trade associations, and with prominent gilds-men sitting as members of the Court of Aldermen, they had every opportunity to flourish. During the mayoralty of Reffham's successor, John de Gisors, a deputation of representatives from all the gilds petitioned the Court of Aldermen that 'the statutes and ordinances regulating the various trades and handicrafts be duly enrolled on a register, and that once or twice a year they be read in public assembly, and copies be delivered to such as desire them', and also that

foreasmuch as the City ought always to be governed by the aid of men engaged in trades and handicrafts, and whereas it was anciently accustomed that no stranger, native or foreign, whose position and character were unknown, should be admitted to the freedom of the City until the merchants and craftsmen, whose business he wished to enter, had previously certified the Mayor and Aldermen of his condition and trustworthiness, the whole Commonalty pray that such observance may be strictly kept for the future as regards the wholesale trades and the handicrafts.[14]

The result of this meeting is not recorded, but when in 1319 Edward II granted the City a new charter, the position of the craft gilds was finally confirmed. The charter enacted that no craftsmen should be made free of the City unless 'on the security of six reputable men of that mistery or craft', and no one should practise a craft unless he was first granted this freedom. This article effectively gave the gilds the right to exercise considerable powers both in their own trades and in the government of the City.

Chapter Two

Trade, Politics and Status

THE charter of 1319 was a landmark in the history of the City and the gilds, and the fourteenth century was a period during which the gilds consolidated their position and did much to extend their control over their own trades. The major crafts, like the Mercers, Grocers, Drapers, and Goldsmiths, whose members were wealthy merchants, were able to extend their influence over City policies so that eventually most Mayors were chosen from their ranks, and so far were they able to exert their power that a practice developed for any ambitious man desirous of making his way in the City to join one of these Companies even if he already belonged to a different trade.

The Brewers did not rank among these leading gilds; although they represented a craft of major importance in the life of all citizens, the same opportunities for amassing great wealth (always a prerequisite of power in the City) were not so easily open to them. Brewing was a domestic craft, and trade with the Continent was virtually non-existent, even after the influx of foreign brewers from the Low Countries. Also, in spite of the value of their product, brewers in general did not have a very good reputation, probably because however essential it might be in moderate quantities, there were many incidents of drunkenness and disturbance as a result of the over-consumption of ale. Ale-houses often had unsavoury reputations, and an article for keeping peace in the City issued in 1310 demanded that 'No taverner keep his tavern open for wine or beer after curfew, nor admit anyone into his tavern, nor into his house, unless he is willing to answer for the King's peace'.[1] It seems that the City was only too well provided with breweries and taverns in the fourteenth and fifteenth centuries (at this period, brewing and retailing were done on the same premises; the wholesale business only developed towards the end of the fifteenth century). The Poll Tax of 1380 indicated that there was approximately one brew-house to every twelve inhabitants!

An examination of the City Letter Books, the main source of information for the history of the City during this period, shows that the Brewers were faced with numerous ordinances against malpractices, particularly selling short measures, which suggest that despite the writ of 1292 the Aldermen and Sheriffs were still prejudiced against them – though probably not entirely unjustifiably! Ordinances regulating the sale of ale and the opening of taverns frequently appeared. In 1316 a proclamation was made that 'no brewer nor brewster nor anyone else sell a gallon of ale for more than 3 farthings and at a penny, and the best at three halfpence. Anyone convicted of doing the contrary shall at the first lose his brew, at the second offence abjure the trade, and at the third abjure the City for ever.'[2] A decree issued by the Mayor and Aldermen in 1352 announced that 'each time that a brewer or brewster sells ale by false measure, the measure shall be burnt and the seller of the ale go to prison and be amerced 25/– for the use of the Commonalty',[3] and in 1378 Aldermen were requested 'to inquire into the misdoings of bakers, brewers, hostelers, masons, carpenters, tilers, daubers and other labourers in their Wards contrary to statute and ordinances, and to make a return of the same to the Chamberlain'.[4] In 1391 the Aldermen were again asked 'to survey the brewers in their several Wards, to see that they sell their ale by sealed measures and that they set a hanap before their customers for them to pour their ale into at will'.[5]

Selling false measure was obviously a common malpractice among brewers, and in 1355 when the ordinances on the sale of ale in recognized measures only were renewed every brewer was also ordered to have his measures approved and sealed by the Aldermen of his Ward. The 'hanap' mentioned in the precept of 1391 was a drinking cup which all taverners were ordered to provide for customers. The ale had to be sold in a sealed measure, and the customer poured it into the hanap. The hanaps were considered a valuable part of a brewer's goods, and on occasions they were confiscated by the Sheriffs and used as a surety when taverners had been caught breaking regulations on the sale of their ale. Attempts were still made to evade the regulations. There is an amusing account of a London ale-wife who was caught selling her brew in the approved quart pots, but these had been filled at the bottom with a layer of pitch; as a penalty she was made 'to play bo pepe thorawe a pillery'.[6]

Such practices did not improve the Brewers' generally low reputation. An interesting piece of evidence as to the unrespectability of the trade is an entry in the first City Letter Book for 1288 concerning regulations for the fur trade, where a complaint was entered that 'brewsters, nurses, other servants and women of disreputable character, adorn themselves and wear hoods furred with gros veer and minever after the manner of reputable women!'[7] Brewers, it seems, were definitely regarded as members of the lower classes, and pretensions to respectability were not encouraged. Their general reputation for all manner of dishonesty provided material for an amusing scene for the author of the morality play *The Harrowing of Hell*. Christ, having redeemed all the souls formerly condemned to hell, finally allows the devil to keep just one soul. It is the soul of a brewer, whose own account of his life made him a fitting companion in eternity for the devil![8]

Because this was the generally accepted view of brewers, those who wished to achieve a position of respectability and influence had a harder task than members of other more highly thought-of trades, even with support of an organized gild. Periodically throughout the fourteenth century they encountered difficulties from being forbidden to take water for their brewing from the Chepe conduit. The case against the Brewers was not without reason; the water supply was limited and a great deal could be used in brewing, thus rendering the supply inadequate for the rest of the inhabitants in the area. The same accusation was made against the Fishmongers. They were first forbidden to use the Chepe in 1310, when the conduit was 'guarded so that brewers and fishmongers shall not use the water thereof'.[9] However, some negotiations must have taken place between the traders and the City authorities, as two years later there is a

Early drinking vessels: leather bottèls, a stoup, and a costrel. *Mansell Collection*

record of money collected from 'brewers, cooks and fishmongers . . . for the easement they enjoy of the water of the conduit in Chepe'.[10] The money thus raised was to be used for necessary repairs to the conduit. This arrangement, however, did not last, and pressure from both sides evidently continued. In 1337 a plea was made at the Court of Hustings that 'the Commonalty were deprived of the water of the Conduit owing to its being so much used by brewers, who carried it away in vessels called tynes',[11] and it was decided that these containers should be confiscated to prevent future abuse. In 1345 the Brewers and Fishmongers were again forbidden to use water from the conduit, but the Brewers at least eventually agreed a compromise with the authorities, whereby they paid for the right to use the upper part of the conduit.[12] It is most probable that negotiations for such rights were made by the corporate body, the gild, on behalf of its members. That the gild was able to achieve eventual success in this is evidence of its growing strength. Soon even greater rights and powers were granted.

Attempts to sell ale at a price above the Assize by claiming inability to give change in farthings was countered by the Aldermen who had supplies of farthings specially distributed to brewers (and bakers) from Guildhall for use as change.[13]

Other entries in the Letter Books of this time show that the Brewers' Gild was gaining a respected status for its members. There is a record of brewers specially appointed by the Mayor to provide and serve ale to King Edward III on his visit to the City in 1356.[14] There is also a note that in 1367 the Brewers contributed £14 6s. 8d. toward a present for the King, a fairly considerable sum; only the leading Goldsmiths gave more.[15] And then to the historic Common Council of 1376 the Brewers' Mistery returned four members, indicating that, after the 'great twelve', the gild was one of the larger ones.[16]

The Common Council of 1376 was of considerable significance in the gradual advance of the gilds, or Misteries as they were generally known, and in the history of the City itself. Common Council, or Common Hall, was a special assembly of citizens called to elect City officers. Originally all freemen were allowed to attend, but as the number increased this became impractical, and by the fourteenth century representatives of the citizens were elected from each Ward to be members of the Council. In the later years of Edward III's reign however there was increasing discontent in the City as some Aldermen had used their position for private gain at the expense of the commonalty, and many citizens demanded that Common Councilmen should be elected by and from the Misteries. This grievance came to a climax in 1376 when three City Aldermen were found guilty before Parliament of serious misconduct for personal profit, and the commonalty petitioned the Mayor and Aldermen for an assembly of men from the leading Misteries to decide the Council's future.

Representatives of forty-one Misteries were summoned to Guildhall – the Brewers were not among these – where it was agreed that

each sufficient mistery should assemble the men of their mistery to elect certain persons against the day when the new Mayor shall be sworn . . . that the persons so elected, and no others, be summoned to elections of Mayors and Sheriffs, and whenever it be necessary to take counsel of the Common-

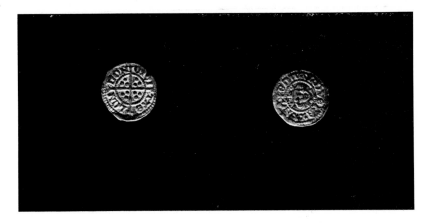

Farthings of Edward II, 1302–10. *British Museum*

alty at the Guildhall, and that each Mistery return the names of those so
elected to the new Mayor on the day of his charge, the greater Misteries
electing not more than six persons, and the rest four or two, according to
their size, for one year.[17]

Thus, government of the City now lay effectively in the hands
of the Misteries, particularly the principal ones, and although
elections by the Wards was returned to in 1384, the Misteries
still maintained a strong influence.

The Brewers named Thomas Potesgrove, John Cook, John
Chipstede and William Strode as their representatives to the
second 1376 Council. W. Herbert in his *History of the Twelve
Great Livery Companies* stated inaccurately that the Brewers
returned five members to this Council and this has led later
writers to over-estimate the importance of the Mistery at this
time.[18] The Brewers were never able to rank on the same footing
as the major gilds, and although their membership was obviously
large, they were clearly not considered of sufficient standing to
be asked to send representatives to the first 1376 Council –
perhaps another indication of their general unpopularity with
the City dignitaries.

In the last years of the fourteenth century the struggle for
power in the City was no longer between Aldermen and craftsmen, but between rival crafts. City politics, however, were often

The true portraicture of *RICHARD WHITINGTON* thrise Lord Maior
of London a vertuous and godly man full of good Works (and those famous) he builded
the Gate of London called Newegate, which before was a miserable doungeon. He builded
Whitington Colledge & made it an Almose house for poore people Also he builded a
greate parte of y hospitall of S.Bartholomewes in westsmithfield in London. He also
builded the beautifull Library at y Gray Friers in Londo, called Christes Hospitall;
Also he builded the Guilde Halle Chappell and increased a greate parte of the East
ende of the saied halle, beside many other good workes.

R. Elstrack Sculpsit

Richard Whitington, bane of the London Brewers. *Guildhall Library,
City of London*

obscured or submerged by events of national dimensions, in which the City played an important part. During the last years of Edward III's reign the war with France, which had been carried on intermittently for almost a century, had resulted in the Crown making increasing demands on the country for money. The City had given considerable loans and gifts, and when Richard II further depleted the exchequer with his extravagance, the City again provided a loan. This, however, could only be a temporary solution, and in 1377 the famous Poll Tax was introduced, which required the sum of fourpence to be paid by every person in the country over the age of fourteen. This proved reasonably successful for the exchequer, though caused some discontent among the populace. When, however, the tax was again levied in 1380, resistance was considerable and culminated in the Peasants' Revolt.

London as the capital and home of the King was the focal point for the rebels, but opinion in the City was divided. Of those who sided with the rebels, however, few did it purely from sympathy with their cause. At the time the City was split within itself by the rival interests of the victualling and the cloth trades (i.e. those trades in which a strict control of imports was advantageous and those whose best interests lay in free trade) and at the time of the peasants' march on London the victuallers' power was rapidly diminishing. They therefore chose to range themselves with the rebels in the hope of regaining status, and, in particular, of gaining a trading monopoly in the City and excluding all foreign traders. There is no evidence as to which side the Mistery of Brewers supported, but it is probable that they sided with other victualling crafts. It is certainly recorded that when a group of rebels marched on the Guildhall threatening to burn it down, they were led by a City brewer, William atte Keye.[19]

The struggle did nothing to further the aims of the victuallers, who suffered a temporary loss of power when John de Northampton, a draper, was elected Mayor in 1381, but the rivalry continued, as did other minor inter-gild disputes, and even quarrels between the 'liveried' members and the journeymen apprentice members of the same gild, as the latter found they were gaining few benefits from their membership. Street fights between rival gilds were not uncommon.[20] Because of the importance of the City in the economic, social and political life of the nation, this continued unrest had wider repercussions than if the same disputes had occurred in a provincial city or town. This is illustrated by the career of Nicholas Brembre, a grocer, leader of the victualling gilds and several times Mayor, who also became one of Richard 11's loyal supporters and advisers, and was eventually found guilty of treason by Parliament in 1388, where a number of leading non-victualling gilds-men testified against him. It was undoubtedly owing to the influence of and rivalry among the leading gilds that in 1389 Parliament instituted an inquiry into the organization of the gilds, their foundation, privileges and property, and any royal charters previously granted had to be handed in for inspection.[21]

Only a few leading Misteries up to this time had obtained royal charters, the Goldsmiths, Skinners, Merchant Taylors, Girdlers, Drapers, Vintners and Fishmongers, and most conferred wide powers and monopolies not only over London but over national trade. None were actually deprived of any of their rights, although it was proved that gilds which owned property did so illegally, but the threat to their powers posed by the inquiry resulted in a general movement to get their association firmly established on a legal basis. This led to the transformation of the gilds into incorporated Livery Companies, the form in which they have survived up to the present day.

The Merchant Taylors were the first to obtain a new charter, which they did in 1390; Goldsmiths, Mercers and Saddlers soon followed. The new charters do not, as the earlier ones, give national trading monopolies to the various crafts, but they constitute each as a perpetual corporate body with the right to a livery, to hold assemblies and make rules for their trade, and to elect a Master and a court of senior men for settling trade disputes, with the right to penalize members. Goldsmiths and Saddlers both obtained the addition of a licence to hold land in mortmain. These rights were all-important to the gilds to allow them to continue unhampered in the control they exercised over their trades, but the charters also made a point of emphasizing the gilds' social and religious purposes, such as assistance offered to needy members. Thus they now encompassed the objects of the original trade gilds and the religious fraternities in one corporation.

At first, the right of incorporation was granted only to the wealthiest and most influential of the gilds, but it was a privilege eagerly sought, and under Henry VI in the 1430s a new group of gilds obtained charters, among them the Brewers (1437), and from then on incorporation became the aim of all the gilds.

Chapter Three

The Company Incorporated

By achieving the status of incorporation in 1437 the Brewers' Gild must have advanced considerably in membership and in their standing in the City. The election of four of their members to the Common Council of 1376 shows that they were among the larger of the minor companies. By 1406 they were able to petition the Mayor and Aldermen for the following rights:

that they may be allowed eight persons of the mistery – four from the east side of Walbrok and four from the west – to wit, two Masters and two Wardens, to rule the mistery and exercise assay, search and survey over all who brew ale within the franchise of the City to sell by wholesale or retail.

Also that those so elected make report to the Chamberlain of the Guildhall for the time being of those brewers, breweresses, hostelers, cooks, pyebakers or hucksters whom they find selling ale otherwise than by sealed measure or at an unlawful price.

Also that no one of the mistery pay a jouneyman more than 3 pence a day and his table between the Feast of St Michael (25 Sept) and the Feast of the Annunciation (25 March), and 4 pence a day and his table between the Feast of the Annunciation and the Feast of St Michael, and if the said journeymen refuse to work on those terms, they may be arrested and brought before the Mayor, Warden or Chamberlain to be punished.

Also that the said Masters and Wardens, eight, six or four of them, may have the power of search and survey of all barley brought to the City for sale, so that it be not broken nor mixed in a sack.

Also that those found rebellious against the said Masters and Wardens may suffer fine and imprisonment according to the ordinance.[1]

These ordinances were duly granted and so the Mistery took upon itself the regulating of its trade, previously laid down and enforced by the Aldermen. And although approval was given on the condition that 'if at any time the Masters and Wardens of the mistery should do anything hurtful, the Mayor or Warden with the consent of the Aldermen should govern and punish offenders in the mistery as theretofore',[2] an echo of low esteem in which the brewing trade had generally been held, the fact that the ordinances were approved indicates that at least the leading members of the craft had improved their status sufficiently to be entrusted with their own regulations. Six months prior to the granting of the above ordinances, the Calendar of Letter Books records a proclamation that 'the Masters of the mistery of Brewers to be allowed to examine all barley brought to the markets at Graschirche and the Pavement before the Friars Minors within Newgate, and to seize all such barley as they find amiss and bring the same before the Mayor and Aldermen',[3] which also points to the Mistery having attained a position worthy of respect.

Having allowed these ordinances, however, the Mayor and Aldermen did not leave the trade entirely within the control of the Mistery. The struggle for power in the previous century encouraged the Aldermen to keep the ultimate control over the activities of the Misteries firmly in their own hands. All ordinances had to be approved by the Court of Aldermen, and new regulations could be issued by them for any trade without the agreement of the Mistery concerned. In 1411 an ordinance was issued by the Mayor forbidding brewers to use hanaps for customers, ordering them to provide instead pewter pots of recognized measure.[4] Of the Brewers' part in this there is no record, but it was undoubtedly another attempt to stop the sale of ale in false measures, and the Mistery's own ordinances declared that the policy of the Court was to punish such abuses. The City authorities, however, obviously thought it necessary to add their own controls over and above those implemented by the Mistery. The balance between the authority of the Mistery and that of the Court of Aldermen seems to have been carefully maintained; clearly neither wished to cross swords with the other, and both relied to a considerable extent on the goodwill of each other to maintain their positions. The Mayor and Aldermen were theoretically in a position to exercise complete control over any Mistery by denying them any self-governing ordinances. In practice, past

Brewing utensils. From the panelling of the Stuart livery hall

events had shown that the support of the Misteries was vital to the maintenance of law and order, and some co-operation was therefore politic. The Misteries for their part also found it advantageous to be on good terms with the City authorities, and in particular the Mayor.

How this worked in practice is well illustrated by the record of how additional ordinances for the Brewers were agreed upon. This is the account as given in the City Letter Books for 1419:

Whereas it had been formerly established that no brewer, hosteler, huckster, cook or pyebaker should sell a gallon of best beer within their houses for more than 2 pence by marked measure, and outside their houses for more than 1½d., many brewers, etc. nevertheless sell a gallon of best beer for 3 pence, 4 pence, and 5 pence, and by 'hanaps', and not by the gallon, 'potel' or quart duly sealed, and, further, they daily make and sell outside their houses, for 1½d. an inferior beer which they sell within their houses, for 2 pence, contrary to the ordinance aforesaid – it was therefore ordained by the said Mayor and Aldermen in this present Common Council that those found acting contrary to the said ordinance shall forfeit their beer and vessels and be committed to prison, the informer getting half of the forfeit.

It was also ordained that this ordinance might be amended by the Mayor and Aldermen in time to come, if it proved to be too rigorous.

The above ordinance was passed by the Mayor and Aldermen, and at the instance of all persons using the mistery of Brewers within the City and suburbs, whose names were submitted to the Court on a roll of paper by the Masters, Wardens, and other good folk of the Mistery.[5]

Later in the same year the Mistery petitioned the Mayor and Aldermen for several amendments to their ordinances granted in 1406, one of which was that 'brewers may be allowed to sell their ale retail in small measure, viz. gallons, potels and quarts, at 2 pence a gallon, as well within their houses as without'.[6] To this the Aldermen refused to consent.

. . . inasmuch as the selling of the best ale outside their houses by retail at 2 pence the gallon would be contrary to the order of the last Common Council, for they must sell their best ale, wholesale or retail, outside their houses at 1½d. the gallon. The Court, however, was willing to modify the penalty imposed at the said Common Council in the following manner, viz. that instead of imprisonment and forfeiture of vessel and value of the ale at every default, the defaulter shall be amerced at the discretion of the Mayor and Aldermen, and this modification is granted on condition that brewers, hostelers, cooks and piebakers sell their ale by full measure in sealed gallons, potels and quarts, and not by hanaps, and do not charge more than 1½d. a gallon for their best ale (the same being sold at 2 pence a gallon within their house) to any one wishing to have more than a gallon.[7]

The wording of both these entries, apart from giving further proof of the efforts made to overcome what was obviously one of the most common malpractices among brewers, shows the nature of the bond between the Mistery and the Court of Aldermen. The first extract states specifically that the ordinances were passed 'at the instance of all persons using the mistery of Brewers' and it is notable that it was agreed that the ordinance could be amended if the Mistery obviously thought that the penalties were too harsh. And indeed the later extract shows that although the Aldermen refused to allow any relaxation in price regulations,

solonc le prus que le mair ou gardein du dit
de mesme la citee ordeignerount en temps
bone able & sayn come deuant est dit. De pʒ
court solonc lour discreacon

¶ Item que les ditz oept sys ou quatre de ciux ʒ
jeconus, braceresses, hostillers, pistbes, pʒ
que pʒ mesure ensenle galon, potell & quart
de la guyhall pur le temps esteaunt de
cion de la courte & enformacion des pʒseit
les ditz meistres & gardeins aloeps du dʒ
oeps de la conustee

¶ Item que null psone deniz le dit mistier loghʒ
ne null de mesme le mistier luy doygne ne
me dame que treys deniers le iour & sa table
que quatre deniers le iour & sa table, sur pey
le resteyuunt doun la quarte ptie tourna
aloeps de la conustee, assint tout dys que pʒ

¶ Item que si la deigne que les psones en sy al
la dite ordeignunce bien lise as ditz oept
deniz la fraunchise du dite citee faire arest
lassueuer su auer gardein ou chaumble
auntz la cause del dit arest assint que si
comitz soyent andetz solonc la distrec
fru come auaunt est dit.

¶ Item que les ditz meistres & gardeins oept si

...le temps esteantz... lassent des Aldermans
...trouent ascune persone fesant cervoise...
...de luy al Chaumbleyn... pur estre punyz...

...les defautes... eux trouez... dit...
...ou hucksters cervoyse vendantz autrement
...cervoise ou outre le pris lymytee al Chaumbleyn
...temps present pur la estre... solonc la...
...qe la quarte partie del fyn fait...
...la remenante a la chaumbre... al

...ordre... ycest mistier...
...peintre le feste de Seint Michell... l'annunciacion
...le dit feste de l'annunciacion... Seint Michell
...fyn a la chaumbre si bien le donant come
...dit mistier... la remenante a la dite chaumbre
...pur euz labourer... le... peine...
...voillent laborer en le mistier avantdit solonc
...de euz ou... quele lieu... les trouent
...de la chaumbre... ces assignee...
...citee pur le temps esteantz pour certifi-
...quant ils... serront resonablement
...informacioun avantditz a departir... le
...atir de euz eyent pouer de faire le cerche...

A folio from Letter Book I. The Letter Books were records of the
daily business of the Guildhall. *By courtesy of the Corporation of London
Record Office*

they did reduce the penalties expected for default. At the same time they consented to two other minor changes in the Brewers' ordinances of 1406. The whole business shows a strong tendency to compromise, with a solution which was acceptable to both sides.

This account from the Letter Books does not, however, give the full story. Most information that has survived concerning the Mistery of Brewers prior to 1418 is found in the Letter Books, the official record of the daily business of the Guildhall. The picture that emerges is inevitably incomplete and, considering the nature of the source, somewhat one-sided. But from 1418 it is possible to refer to the Brewers' own records. William Porland's Minute Book, which covers the period 1418–40, is the oldest of its kind to survive among the records of the City Livery Companies, and provides a wealth of information on the day-to-day activities of the Mistery. The first page explains its purpose:

This paper, first written, the month of November, in the Sixth year of the reign of King (Henry v) after the conquest of England, maketh full remembrance and understanding of all the Receipts and Expenses made by the Masters for the time being of the Fraternity and Mistery of the Brewers of the City of London, founded in the parish church of All Saints in London Wall: – William Sevenoke then Mayor of the same City, John Perneys and [Ralph] Barton Sheriffs of the same City; and William atte Wode, William Edriche, William Ferrour and John Reyner being also the Masters of the Fraternity aforesaid. And in this year died John Morey then Clerk of the same Brewers, to wit, the tenth day of the month of February, in the sixth year abovesaid. And the fourteenth day of the same month of February, William Porland was taken to the same office, to be Clerk of the said Brewers; and the said William ordained this book, to have cognizance of all the things done in the Mistery and Fraternity abovesaid, for all the time that the said William should be Clerk of the said Brewers.[8]

There is much of a purely domestic nature in the book concerning the Mistery's internal affairs, but it also includes many references to the Brewers' relationship with the City authorities. From Porland's account of the disputed 1419 ordinances, it appears that the Mayor, at least, was firmly opposed to the Brewers, and co-operation with the Court of Aldermen was not easy. The Mayor at the time was the legendary Richard Whitington, and he seems to have waged a personal war against the

William Porland's Minute Book. *Guildhall Library*

Brewers during his period of office. Prior to the reaffirmation of the ordinance on the use of sealed measures for the sale of ale, Porland records that Whitington took offence against the Brewers 'for their having fat swans at their feast on the morrow of St Martin'[9] and as a result proclaimed that brewers had to sell beer cheaply, at 1d. a gallon, all the following day. When later this ordinance was modified, Porland's record of the petition by the Brewers refers to the earlier decrees as 'certain grievous Statutes set forth in the time of the said Mayor against the Craft of Brewers.'[10]

This, however, was not the end of the dispute with Whitington, though the following incidents are not mentioned in the Letter Books. In 1421 Porland records another 'most violent and tyrannical attempt by Whitington to oppress and extort money from the Brewers of London'. The account is lengthy, but the main points are as follows:

He [Whitington] summoned all the Huksteres in the city [women retailing ale and beer] to appear at Guildhall, and there inquired on oath the prices at which they bought and sold their beer and the names of the Brewers that supplied them, all which being recorded in the Chamberlain's book, those Brewers were summoned on the 22nd of August, and, on examination, their prices corresponded with the Huksteres' statement; but the Mayor declared them false, and grievous transgressors; and that they had incurred the penalty of £20. . . . For a long time they nobly refused to submit to the extortion of the Mayor, who continually urged them to pay the sum with violent threats. He passed a resolution in the Common Council that if they did not submit to his will, the whole company should be undone and dissolved.

Offers to pay part of the sum were utterly refused, but the Brewers were finally able to postpone payment until after Whitington's term of office had expired, when the Masters approached the new Mayor, William Cambrugge, who required them only to pay £10, and the rest 'when they could conveniently collect it'.[11]

It would seem that the Brewers' difficulties with the authorities at this period were the result of Whityngton's personal animosity rather than the united opposition of the Aldermen. This appears most clearly in Porland's account of the last of the Mistery's struggles with Whitington, which occurred after his term as

Mayor. On 30 July 1422 the Masters and twelve other members of the Mistery were summoned to Guildhall and accused of selling ale above the Assize.

After much altercation on the price and quality of malt, wherein Whityngton declared that the Brewers had ridden into the country and forestalled the malt to raise its price, they were convicted in the said penalty, and the Masters were ordered to be kept in prison in the Chamberlain's custody, until they should pay it or find surety for the payment. When the Mayor and Aldermen had gone homeward to their meat, the Masters went and asked the Chamberlain and Clerk what they should do, who bid them go home, promising that no harm should come to them, for all this proceeding had been done but for to please Richard Whityngton, for he was cause of all the foresaid Judgement.[12]

Fortunately for the Brewers, other Mayors were better disposed towards the Mistery. Whitington's successor William Cambrugge (or Cambrigge) on Porland's evidence treated them well and 'gave them good advice, which they were pleased with';[13] Mayor Robert Chichele also treated the Brewers well. It was naturally an advantage to have a Mayor who would not trouble the Mistery with restrictions and fines, and, presumably having learnt from their battles with Whitington, the Brewers were not averse to a little bribery. When William Walderne (Mayor 1422–3) showed signs of making trouble, the Company 'assuaged his displeasure by presenting to him, a Boar, price 20s. and an Ox price 17s'.[14] The same gifts were made to John Michelle when he was elected Mayor 'so that he did no harm to the Brewers, and advised them to make good ale, that he might not have complaints against them'.[15]

The grant of a royal charter, however, made the Mistery less vulnerable to attack by the City authorities. The Company still has this charter, dated 22 February 1437. The rights which it gave are stated briefly and simply:

Henry, by the grace of God King of England and France and Lord of Ireland. To all to whom the present shall come Greeting. Know that we of our special grace have granted and given licence for us and our heirs to the Freedom of the Mystery of Brewers of the City of London that they hereafter be in deed and name one Body and perpetual Commonalty and that the same Commonalty be able every year to elect and make from among themselves four Wardens to supervise rule and govern and punish all the

The charter of incorporation granted to the Company by Henry VI,
dated 22 February 1437. *Guildhall Library*

men of the same Mistery and Commonalty hereafter for ever. And also all workmen and production of any liquor whatsoever from malt to be sold or made in the City aforesaid and in the suburbs of the same. And that the same Wardens and Commonalty have perpetual succession and a common seal to serve for the business of the said Mystery and Commonalty. And that the same Wardens and Commonalty by the name of the Wardens and Commonalty of the Mistery of Brewers of the City of London be able to plead and be impleaded before any judges whomsoever in any courts whatsoever. And that also the same Wardens and Commonalty and their successors forever be persons able in law to acquire and possess in perpetuity lands tenements rents and other possessions whatsoever of any persons whomsoever. And in particular that they be able to acquire lands tenements and rents in London to the value of 10 marks per year, to have and hold to them and their successors to help the sustenance of the poor men and women of the Mistery and Commonalty aforesaid.[16]

Such rights, authorized by royal charter, were of great benefit to the Mistery. Porland records that the 'expenses made for the Charter of the capacity for the craft of Brewers of London' amount to £141 2s. 0d.[17] but this must have been considered money well spent. The municipal authorities were not idle in their attempts to combat some of the charters granted at this time, which diminished their control over the Misteries thus incorporated as they obtained the right to draw up their own ordinances. An Act of Parliament passed in 1437 required that all such charters should be submitted to the town hall to be registered. The Brewers' charter was immediately questioned, and they were required to promise obedience to the Court of Aldermen. One of the last entries in Porland's book notes that 27s. 4d. was paid 'to get to us friendship for to have our Charter confirmed by the Parliament',[18] and in this the Brewers seem to have fared better than some of the other Misteries. The Merchant Taylors, who obtained a new charter in 1439, immediately lost the rights granted therein when the Mayor and Aldermen demanded its withdrawal. Even with a charter, a gild had to obtain the approval of the Mayor before its ordinances could be enforced, so to be on good terms with those in office was still advantageous.

However, it appears that after this grant of royal charter, the Brewers were less harried than previously. Ordinances concerning their trade no longer have the look of 'vexatious statutes', and the effective control was more in the hands of the Master and Wardens than with the Mayor and Aldermen. This is clear from the terms of an ordinance issued by the Mayor in 1453, which requires that brewers 'make their vessels according to the assize, and have them stamped with their own iron marks, which marks are to be recorded in the Chamber, under penalty prescribed; and further, that they sell their beer at prices pre-cribed and by sealed measures "full of clier bere wythoute vyall" '.[19] In other words, the Brewers were responsible for making their own vessels of approved sizes, and these had no longer to be sealed by the Aldermen. The status of the Company had achieved a tacit acknowledgement, even if there were still plenty of brewers only too ready to make a little extra profit by dishonest means.

Chapter Four

Clerical Memoranda

WILLIAM PORLAND'S Minute Book, referred to in the previous chapter, affords a quantity of interesting information on both the domestic affairs of the Brewers' Company and some of the notable public events of the period. Because of its unique character it is worth while considering in some detail.

The book is not in exact chronological order, as Porland seems to have turned back to make use of blank spaces as the pages were gradually filled up, but most entries are dated, so some chronological order emerges. Porland uses the three languages in common usage at the time, Latin, Norman French and Middle English, apparently indiscriminately. Latin had, of course, been established for centuries as the language of the educated classes. It was the language of the Church, and as in the early Middle Ages the clergy were the only men generally able to read and write, it became also the recognized language of government and communication. Norman French was introduced in England at the time of the conquest, and being the language of the ruling class, also became established as an official language of government. But to the greater part of the population both these languages were unintelligible; all their affairs were conducted in English, and the dialect could vary considerably in different parts of the country.

However, in the early years of the fifteenth century it was unusual for any official records to be kept in English, and the vernacular passages in Porland's book are some of the earliest extant examples of written London English. Porland made a note of his reasons for using English and entered it in the book:

Whereas our Mother tongue, to wit the English tongue, hath in modern days begun to be honourably enlarged and adorned, for that our most excellent lord, King Henry v, both in his letters missive and divers affairs touching his own person, more willingly chosen to declare the secrets of his will, and for the better understanding of his people, hath with a diligent mind procured the common idiom (setting aside others) to be commended by the exercise of writing – and there are many of our Craft of Brewers who have the knowledge of writing and reading in the said English idiom, but in others, to wit, the Latin and French, before these times used, they do not in anywise understand. For which causes with many others it being considered now that the greater part of the Lords and trusty Commons have begun to make their matters be noted down in our mother tongue; so we also, in our craft, following in some manner their steps, have decreed in future to commit to memory the needful things which concern us.[1]

Following this the records continue mainly in English, but there are some subsequent items in Latin, and it is amusing to find that the above paragraph itself was in fact written in Latin!

The entries in the book are mixed; records of events important to the Company are interspersed with business-like accounts, lists of members paying quarterage, and those fined for malpractices, and menus and costs of dinners held in the Company's hall.

It is uncertain when the Brewers first acquired a hall of their own. By the fifteenth century it had become the practice of all Livery Companies who could afford it to have their own hall for their business and for social events. The Brewers built theirs on a site in Addle Street, leased from the Dean and Chapter of St Paul's. The first mention of a 'Brewers Hall' is found in the Chapter's records of 1403, and in 1419 the 'unanimous assent of all the Masters of the Brewers Craft, licensed and granted to William Porland common clerk of the Craft aforesaid, to his wife, children and servants, free and quiet dwelling in the hall of the company commonly called Brewers Halle, with the use of the chamber, and of other utensils and necessaries belonging to the said hall'.[2]

Members of the Company met at the hall every Monday to conduct their business, but the building was also let to other Companies who had no hall of their own. One of the first

Henry v, by an unknown artist. *National Portrait Gallery*

entries in Porland's book is a note of rent paid by the Companies of Glovers, Master-Clerks, Coopers, Masons and Pointmakers for use of the hall. Very curiously it also appears that the hall was let on three occasions to the Footballplayers, and at a charge of 1s. 4d. they seem to have had it cheaper than others![3] This is one of the earliest mentions of football in English, and there was certainly no Livery Company of Footballers; such games were generally forbidden at this time as leading to rowdyism. They are not mentioned again, and do not appear in Porland's list of the 'Divers crafts in the City of London' which numbers 111, and which are noted 'in case that they may in any manner be of advantage to the Hall and Company of Brewers'.[4] Some of the crafts named are quite odd, many were obviously very small organizations, and in time these tended to amalgamate with other allied crafts to improve their status and prosperity so that they could eventually buy a charter.

In 1423 it was agreed that 'the tenement nigh our great gate' should be made 'an Almshouse for the poor brethren and sisters of the craft', and one of the masters, Robert Smyth, gave £10 'to part it into divers chambers and for repairs and fitting up'.[5] Porland records the various expenses for this work and for other repairs and improvement to the hall itself, which was likely 'to have fallen down in default of reparation'. Among works carried out he mentions:

> Timber and carpentry, for the making of a 'tresauns' sometimes called the Cloister between the great kitchen and the Hall.
> Tiling from the Hall door inward; for all the houses in our place were pointed new as in tiling – except the body of the great hall.
> An 'Almanie' [cupboard] that standeth in the great kitchen.
> A hen coop in the yard.[6]

The major work, however, was the installation of a 'Bay-wendowe' like one in Cornhill. For the work the Company employed one John Pekkere, a carpenter of Cambridge, who it appears charged them excessively, in spite of being given a cloth gown by the Masters, and so was given no further work by the Company. Below the list of costs for the work, there is an entry for 16d. paid to 'a Taker of the King's, for to suffer our carpenters still in their work', to stop the workmen being pressed into the King's service, a common occurrence at the time.[7]

Two years later, other repairs were carried out including 'The making of the chamber that was broken with thunder' and 'amending a kitchen by our place, for dread of fire', for which the charge was 14s. 6½d.[8]

The costs of such works were presumably paid out of the quarterage paid by members. An annual list of those who paid was usually recorded, likewise the names of those who failed to pay. There are also lists recording the admission of new freemen to the Company, and attached to the Masters' Accounts for 1419 is a note of what the Masters contributed to the funds:

For every free man admitted that year to the freedom of the Brewers' craft, 6s. 8d., and for every brother admitted to the fraternity 3s. 4d., according to an ancient custom ordained and approved by the unanimous consent of the Brethren, as it appeareth in an ancient paper with a red calf-skin cover, in the fourth quire and first leaf; and for good example and information to future successors, to be regarded and observed.[9]

In 1429 this practice was called in question and no record enforcing the custom could be found. It was agreed that subsequently every person admitted to the freedom should pay 28s. 6d., half of which should go to the Company's common funds, the rest to the Masters.[10]

The 'fraternity' probably refers to those members entitled to wear the livery. New cloth for livery gowns was bought annually; in 1419 the colour was green and the total cost was £185 4s. 10d., a considerable sum. Members paid for their livery gowns, but the Masters and the Clerk had theirs free. In 1421 Porland recorded that 'in consequence of the grievances and great charges imposed on the Company by Richard Whityngton all the year of his mayoralty the Brewers refused to make feasts or breakfasts, or to provide their yearly livery'.[11] In 1429 it was decided that the election of new Masters and selection of a new livery should be made every two years in future.[12] It appears that this was to allay the dissatisfaction of younger members who had been protesting about the dominance of the Company by older men. How the election of new Masters every two years should remedy the situation is not clear, however!

Dinners and feasts were held regularly, also breakfasts, which seem to have been popular on account days. Porland records many of the menus and costs of these affairs, some of which make entertaining reading.

In 1425 the Company spent £38 on its election day feast. The bill for the main items runs as follows:

> 21 Swans – 3s. 9d. each
> Poultry – £8
> 2 Geese – 8d. each
> 40 Capons – 6d. each
> 40 Conies – 3d. each
> 48 Partridges – 4d. each
> 12 Woodcocks – 4d. each
> 12½ doz. Smaller birds – 6d. per dozen
> 3 doz. Plovers – 3s.
> 18 doz. Larks – 4d. per doz.
> 6 doz. Little birds – 1½d. per doz.[13]

On this occasion all Freemen paid 12d. to attend, women paid 8d. and husband and wife together 20d. For preparing the meal the cook was paid 23s., six turnspits and four assistants had 3d. each. For an entertainment at the feast players and two harpists received £5 0s. 10d. It was quite common for some form of entertainment to be provided between the substantial courses of a medieval banquet; usually it was in the form of an 'Interlude', a medieval version of a one-act play, which would include music, singing and sometimes dancing. Among the expenses noted for a dinner in 1435 is the item 'payed to four Clerkis of London for a Play – 5s. 4d.'.[14]

Breakfasts seem to have been provided from the common funds. On one occasion a member, one William Payne, refused to contribute a barrel of ale to be sent to the King during his campaigns in France, and he was fined 3s. 4d. to provide a swan for the Masters' breakfast. Simon Potken was also made to pay for a swan for the Masters. He had given 20s. to a fund to be used to get Mayor Whitington's oppressive ordinances modified. He was later fined by the Aldermen for selling his ale in short measure, whereat he informed the City Chamberlain that he had paid a sum to the Masters of the Brewers' Company in return for permission to sell at his own will. 'For this slander he got into great trouble, and was fined 3s. 4d. for a swan to be eaten by the Masters, but he had his share.'[15]

It was not unusual for demands for goods in kind to be provided for the King in times of war, both for the army and for his own household. Such supplies were paid for by the exchequer, though frequently at a cut price. In 1422 Porland records money 'received of the Treasurers of England, for Ale delivered by divers Brewers of the City of London, to the household of Lady Katherine the Queen, after the passage of King Henry v last made into the parts of France'.[16]

In 1435 there was a special levy of money made to help in the defence of Calais, and the Brewers' book lists those members who 'did pay divers parcels of money to help wage soldiers for to keep Calais, when the Duke of Burgundy came to besiege the said town'. The total collected was £13 3s. 6d.[17]

The Company sometimes made special levies to cover extraordinary expenses; the petition against Whitington's ordinances was one such occasion. The sum raised, by what Porland calls a 'voluntary taxation', for the petition to Common Council against these ordinances was £31 7s. 4d., and the account of how the money was used is curious, indicating the importance of obtaining influential friends in the right places. The money was divided thus: '£20 to Robert Whetyngham, Sheriff: £7 3s. 4d. for 2 pipes of Red Wine to Richard Whityngton's butler: 20s. to John Carpenter the Mayor's Clerk: 32s. for 2 butts of Malmsey wine to Tho. Fakonere, Alderman and Recorder: Porterage 6s. 8d.: Writing of the Petition 6d. Spent in collecting the money 6d.: Left for common use 40s. 4d.'[18]

The Company's funds were continually needed at this time for petitions to protest against the poor quality and high price of malt, and also the activities of foreign brewers. A petition, undated, but possibly drawn up in 1422–3, against the maltmen, was presented 'unto the wise and discrete person the Speaker of the Parliament, and the worthy Commons of the Realm',[19] and later a similar appeal was addressed to the King himself. In 1436 there was a special petition 'unto the right worshipful and gracious lord and sovereigns, the Mayor and Aldermen of the City of London, stating the distress occasioned to the Brewers by a great dearth of malt and begging therefore to be released from "the common fine" yearly imposed on them to be paid into the Guildhall, which would be to them full importable to bear'.[20]

Some expenses incurred in 1438 throw light on the Company's continued links with the Church. The early existence of a religious Fraternity of Brewers has already been mentioned. By the early fifteenth century the fraternity had merged with the more openly trade-based Mistery of Free Brewers, for the opening paragraph of Porland's book refers clearly to 'the Fraternity and Mistery of the Brewers of the City of London, founded in the parish church of All Saints in London Wall'. The connection with All-Hallows Church continued, and quarterage lists usually distinguish between members who were freemen of the Company, and those 'brethren' who were also members of the fraternity. Alms were paid out in the name of the fraternity, and undoubtedly the Company had its own Masses and services at All-Hallows Church, just as many other companies maintained connections with other City churches, some of which have survived into the twentieth century.

In 1438, however, the Lord Mayor requested the Brewers to transfer their allegiance from All-Hallows to the Church of Aldermanbury, in which parish the Company's hall stood. Porland records the expenses connected with the change, including 'money payed to the succeeding Masters for standing out of office 8 weeks when our offering was translated from All-Hallows in the Wall to the Church of Aldermanbury'. Why the new Masters should have had to stand down while this move was completed is not known, but they received £4 13s. 4d. between them for the favour.[21]

Sometimes Parliament ordered the Livery Companies to provide money for certain 'public services', and Porland has a detailed account of one such occasion, of which the following is a summary:

The king held his Parliament on the 2nd May 1422, and it was decreed that all the weirs or 'kydells' in the Thames between Stanes and Gravesend and Queensburgh should be destroyed for the commonalty of the City of London should have the more plenty of fish. Whereupon the Mayor called a Common Council, and it was ordained that two men from each of 26 crafts should go out with the Mayor on this business. With the Brewers were

The Church of St Mary, Aldermanbury. *Guildhall Library*

joined 6 other crafts, the Girdlers, Fletchers, Salters, Barbers, Dyers and Tallow Chandlers, to go in one barge, but the Fletchers excused themselves, as being too busy in preparing artillery for the king, and were permitted to find substitutes and make payment. The Brewers chose Thomas Grene and Roger Swannefeld to go up to Kingston, who spent 13s. 4d. and Robert Carpenter and John Mason to go to Gravesend, who spent 20s. each having a reward of 6s. 8d. They moreover payed to the Chamberlain 50s. for 3 workmen for 28 days, and by order of the Mayor, levied a tax on the craft for this purpose, which was with difficulty collected.[22]

The Brewers, along with the Mayor, Aldermen and other Livery Companies were expected to take part in the royal

Engraving of Brewers' Hall, Addle Street, rebuilt after the Great Fire of 1666. By Thomas Shepherd

processions which accompany any visit by the sovereign to the City. When Henry v returned from France in 1422

William Cambrigge, the Mayor, rode with all the commonalty of the city to meet him, who were all commanded to be clad alike in white gowns with red capes. The Brewers ordered that all householders of their company and all Brewersmen of 40s. a year, should provide clothes for themselves under fine of 20s. but many neglected and yet were let off easily. William the Clerk had a gown given him by the Masters.[23]

The obligation of turning out and providing themselves with gowns for such occasions was obviously not always popular, and in 1434 Porland notes names of those 'that made divers fines for to be excused of their riding when King Henry vi did come out of France from his Coronation in France'.[24]

Undoubtedly the greatest public spectacle during Porland's

period as Clerk must have been Henry v's funeral. The Brewers seem to have paid up handsomely on this occasion, which is described in detail, and probably with some pride, by Porland:

William Waldern was chosen Mayor on S. Edwards Day when it was ordered that the Aldermen and Crafts should wear black and go to Westminster with him to take his charge, in barges without minstrels. Every able householder was charged to provide a black or russet gown and a black hood, and after the charge to be present at the King's funeral.

Certain crafts were ordered to find 200 torches for the funeral, and the Brewers provided eight, weighing 138lb. of wax price 51s. 9d.

The Chamberlain gave white gowns to the torch-bearers and the Brewers paid to each 3d. a day for 2 days. The royal corpse was brought to London on Thursday 5th November and was met at Saint Georges bar in Southwark by the Mayor, Sheriffs and citizens, on foot; the Brewers stood at St Margarets Churchyard until the funeral procession had gone by, (preceded by the torchbearers) and then followed to St Pauls, where a dirige was performed. On the next day several masses were sung by many bishops and others, who after eating, led the corpse to Westminster, with the Mayor etc. The torches were held at the gate of the Abbey, until all had entered; and when brought back weighed 112lb. and were sold for 28s. Every householder from the Church of St Magnus to Temple Bar had a servant holding a torch at his door, while the procession passed. The burial was solemnised on Saturday 7th November when there were offered at the high altar 4 steeds royally trapped, with a knight full and whole armed with the king's coat-armour, and a crown upon his head, sitting on one of the steeds – after Mass 200 cloths of gold were offered.[25]

It is impossible to recount in detail everything chronicled by Porland but from the selection quoted in this chapter it is possible to get quite a clear picture of the state of the Brewers' Company in the early fifteenth century, its major concerns and daily business. The book is a continuous record of the years 1418 to 1441, when Porland died. The exact date of his death is uncertain, but under a heading 'Wages' at the end of the book, there is the entry: 'To Robert Cokat, Clerk of the same Craft, for 3 quarters of the said year, 30s. Item to the wife late of Will. Porland for her pension by the said year, 40s.'[26] It is remarkable, however, that there does not seem to be any change in the handwriting for this item, or in the three remaining pages in the book. It is difficult to speculate on the possible reasons for this, but Porland must certainly have been dead when the above entries were made.

Chapter Five

The Extension of Power

No detailed records such as those kept by Porland have survived from the latter years of the fifteenth century, but such evidence as exists shows that the Brewers consolidated the position they had won for themselves. At this time the Livery Companies were reaching the height of their power and influence. Members of the leading Companies were regularly elected as Aldermen, and such disputes as arose were no longer between the Companies and the City authorities but rather between individual Companies for position and privilege.

The advance of the Companies till they ranked as the major power in the City is shown through the gradual domination they gained in the Court of Common Council. Originally all citizens were summoned to Common Hall to elect the important officers of the City. By the fourteenth century, Guildhall being too small for such a large assembly, attendance was limited to notable citizens representing each Ward. In 1467 the Masters and Wardens of the Misteries were also summoned to attend, and then in 1475 attendance was limited to liverymen only, a privilege that they have retained to the present day and which was confirmed by statute in 1725. It was also established that a person could only become a freeman of the City through membership of a gild. The freedom was a valuable thing to attain; it was considered essential for anyone following a trade in the City, and carried with it certain privileges such as freedom from impressment into the army. That it could only be attained through membership of a Livery Company confirmed the strong position of the Companies both in their individual trades and in the government of the City.

The Brewers' Company, having obtained its charter, proceeded to exercise the right of control in the trade, endeavouring to suppress those dishonest practices which had done much to bring brewing into disrepute in former years. But the Brewers' main concern at this time was to eliminate foreign competition and oppose the introduction of hopping beer. The two problems were interrelated, for it was the foreign traders who settled in London during the late fourteenth and fifteenth centuries who introduced the brewing of beer with hops. These immigrants, mostly from Flanders and Holland, settled mainly around the South Bank. Here they were near the City, and had the use of the Thames for trade and communication; but they were not subject to the restrictions imposed within the City boundaries on foreign traders.

The Brewers' Company sought ordinances from the Mayor and Aldermen both against the foreign brewers and their beer. The City Letter Book for 1484 records:

Came good men of the Art of Brewers into the Court of the lorde the King in the Chamber of the Guildhall, before Robert Billesdone, the Mayor, and the Aldermen, and presented a petition praying that no maner of persone of what craft condicion or degree he be occupying the craft or fete of bruyng of ale within the saide Cities or libertie thereof from hensforth occupie or put or do or suffre to be occupied or put in any ale or licour whereof ale shal be made or in the wirkyng and bruyng of any maner of ale any hoppes herbs or other like thing but onely licour malt and yeste under penalty prescribed,[1]

and on this occasion the petition was granted, for the Brewers were not the only ones to suffer from foreign competition and there was a general opposition to foreign traders in the City. In 1463 a statute forbade the import of foreign goods, in order to encourage and protect native trades. The use of hops was a foreign practice and as such to be condemned. A petition was made to Parliament to forbid the 'use of the wicked weed in beer', and every opportunity was taken to condemn the use of hops as being 'to the great deceit and hurt of the King's liege people'.[2] So opposed were the ale-brewers to the foreign beer-brewers that a statute of Edward VI forbade the two different crafts to unite, and stated that beer-brewers should not be forced to be members of the Brewers' Company.

Towards the end of the fifteenth century, however, the use of hops seems to have become accepted; evidence for this being found in a petition made to the Mayor and Aldermen by the 'berebrewers' in 1493. The use of hops is specifically mentioned in two clauses:

> That no one of the Craft send any wheat, malt or other grain for brewing to the mill to be ground, not put any hops in the brewing unless it be clean and sweet, under penalty of 20s....
>
> That the said Rulers, with an officer of the Chamber appointed for the purpose, shall search all manner of hops and other grain four times a year or more, and taste and assay all beer.[3]

These references imply that the ban on hops was no longer in force. It has also indicated that the beer-brewers had established a gild of their own. The entry in the Letter Book specifically states that the petition was made by the 'berebrewers', whereas elsewhere the Brewers' Company are referred to as simply the Brewers.

An earlier entry for 1464 confirms this. It is a petition by the 'berebrewers' for ordinances, and states: 'for the brewers of Bere as yet been none ordenaunces nor rules by youre auctorites made for the comon wele of the saide Citee for the demeanyng of the same Mistiere of Berebrewers', and it continues: 'Forasmuche as they have not ordenaunces ne rules set among theym like as other occupacions have it is surmysed upon theym that often tymes they make theire Bere of unseasonable malt the which is of litle prise and unholsome for mannes body for theire singular availe, forasmuche as the comon people for lacke of experience can not knowe the perfitnesse of Bere aswele as of the Ale.'[4]

The beer-brewers were granted their ordinances as a separate gild, but it could not have flourished long. There are no further references to it in the Letter Books, and the use of hops in beer was banned again under Henry VIII, and remained so until the end of Edward VI's reign, by which time the ale-brewers were finding the advantage to be gained from it.

Even the City authorities quickly recognized that the increased number of foreign traders in and around the City was not wholly undesirable. Competition from the newcomers could be used as an effective means of ensuring that native craftsmen kept their prices from rising too high. In 1478 a decree by the Common Council announced that 'inasmuch as brewers of the City enhance the price of beer against the Common weal, foreign brewers should come into the City, and there freely sell their beer until further order'.[5]

It was a source of much discontent among not only the Brewers that the foreigners were able to practise their trade freely in Southwark, where craftsmen were beyond the jurisdiction the gilds exercised over their own trade within the City. Within the City boundaries the powers of the gilds were now extensive; the City Letter Books for the latter half of the fifteenth century are full of requests to the Mayor and Aldermen for additional ordinances giving the Companies more control over their trades, and it was perhaps as well that the ever-present threat of competition from without prevented a completely despotic rule. For the success of the foreign traders in spite of City opposition showed that membership of a gild was not essential to a craftsman's well-being, and so if the rule of the gilds became too oppressive, he had only to move to the other side of the Thames to escape it. The ordinances which the 'Wardens and good men of the Craft of Brewers' were granted in 1482 show how far the Company had extended its powers, for these 'articles for the regulation of the Craft' cover a variety of matters; some of the rights mentioned had already been granted to the Company, but here, for the first time, they were set out together.

The articles were as follows:

That every person occupying the craft of brewing within the franchise make, or cause to be made, good and 'hable' ale, according in strength and fineness to the price of malt for the time being; that no ale after it be 'clensed and sett on jeyst' be put to sale or carried to customers until it have fully 'spourged' and been tasted and viewed by the Wardens of the Craft or their Deputy, according to the ordinances and customs of the City; and that the taster allow no ale that is not 'holesome for mannys body', under penalty of imprisonment and a fine.

That ale be not sent out in other men's vessels without leave of the owners of the vessels.

The first grant of arms to the Company, 23 July 1468, with the hanging seal of William Hawkeslowe, Clarenceux King-of-Arms. *Guildhall Library*

That no brewer maintain a foreyn to retail his ale within the franchise of the City.

That no brewer entice customers of another occupying the same craft.

That no brewer engage a Typler or Huxster to retail his ale until he be sure that the said Typler or Huxster is clearly out of debt and danger for ale to any other person occupying the craft of brewing within the franchise.

That no Typler or Huxster lend, sell, break or cut any barrel, kilderkin or ferkin belonging to any other brewer without leave of the owner.

That every person keeping a house and being a Brother of Bruers and occupying the craft of brewing pay quarterage towards the great charges and cost of the Craft and Fraternity.

That no one of the Craft, whether he be in the livery of the same or not, presume to go and dine at the feasts of the Mayor or Sheriffs when they are presented at Westminster, unless appointed by the Wardens to take the place of one unable to attend.

That every freeman of the craft obey the summons of the Wardens on all occasions, under penalty of a fine, except for reasonable cause.

That at every third year, on the election of new Wardens of the Craft and Fraternity, the men of the livery shall attend in a new gown and hood and hear Mass at the Church of St Mary in Aldermanbury, or such other place as may be assigned, and also attend the dinner in the Common Hall of the Fraternity; that every such person keep the said livery for the space of six years next ensuing for divers assemblies of the Fellowship; that if he fail to attend in his livery on any occasion, without reasonable excuse, he be fined; that if he receive from the Wardens an example or pattern of the livery, and so be licensed to provide and buy his cloth for the said livery where he pleases, and the colour of the cloth so bought and provided be not according to the colour of the said example, he be also fined.

That once every quarter all members of the Fellowship attend, on summons, at the Common Hall of the said Craft or Fellowship, to hear read the statutes and ordinances approved and enacted by the Mayor and Aldermen for the good rule of the Craft, in order that no one incur penalties through ignorance of them.

That no brewer take any servant that has not served his time as an apprentice to the craft, and been made a freeman of the City; nor keep in his house at one time more than two or three apprentices at the most, that all such apprentices be first presented to the Wardens in the Common Hall of the Craft, and by them be publicly examined as to their birth, cleanliness of their bodies and other certain points.

That apprentices be presented to the Wardens by their master before admission to the freedom of the City, so that it may be ascertained whether they have duly served their term; and that no apprentice who has served his term shall become a Chief brewer or Under brewer, and therefore take wages, until certified as able by the said Wardens under penalty prescribed.[6]

The extension of control exercised by the Companies over their trade and their members led also to the gradual evolvement of a governing body of senior men in each Company, the Court, to assist the Wardens. Prior to this, a Company had been under the sole control of its Wardens, of which there were usually four. The title of Master at this time denoted a master craftsman and was not used specifically for the senior officers of the Company. The petition made by the Brewers in 1493, already mentioned above, included a request which indicates that such a body of senior men was beginning to form.

Two persons submitted to them may be admitted as Wardens of the Fellowship for the ensuing year, and be sworn in the Court of the Guildhall, called the Mayor's Court, to rule the Craft and see that its ordinances are observed, and that henceforth the Rulers and Governors of the Fellowship before going out of office, calling into them 6 or 8 honest members, shall choose Rulers and Governors for the following year.[7]

The large number of members of the Company would have made it impossible for the Wardens alone to ensure that all the ordinances for the trade were being obeyed. The City Letter Book for 1420 recorded the names of 300 members of the Brewers' Company, twenty of whom were women.[8]

Women had always been admitted to gild membership; though it was natural that while some had quite a number of women, others had none admitted in their own right, though it was customary to admit widows of freemen to their husbands' gilds. The Brewers' female membership, as many as thirty-nine in 1417, was unusually high, for women were commonly involved in brewing on a domestic scale. But the much larger male membership of the Company would seem to refute the accepted view that up to the end of the fifteenth century, brewing in the City was done almost entirely by women. This supposition probably arose from the large number of 'ale-wives' in the City. These women, however, were usually only retailers, owners of small ale-houses who bought their ale from one of the larger brewers, some of whom were beginning to enter the wholesale trade. Also, the title of ale-wife was not synonymous with hukster or hostess at this time, the latter being mainly sellers of wine, whose houses were known as taverns. Such a one was Shakespeare's Mistress Quickly, hostess of the Boar's Head Tavern, Eastcheap, and in her efforts to maintain a semblance of order among Falstaff's band of followers, she recounts this interview with the 'deputy'. Ale-houses and taverns generally had poor reputations as places of brawls and rowdyism, which the law made repeated endeavours to control:

I was before Master Tisick, the deputy, t'other day; and, as he said to me, – 'twas no longer ago than Wednesday last, – 'Neighbour Quickly,' says he; – Master Dumbe, our minister, was by then; – Neighbour Quickly,' says he, 'receive those that are civil, for, said he, 'you are in an ill name;' now, a' said so, I can tell whereupon; 'for,' says he, 'you are an honest woman, and well thought on; therefore take heed what guests you receive: receive,' says he, 'no swaggering companions.'[9]

The second grant of arms. *Guildhall Library*

Taverns and ale-houses were distinguished for the passer-by by the ale-stake. It has already been mentioned that roadside ale-houses were distinguished by a long pole hung above the door. The practice was certainly current in London, and an ordinance of 1292 limited the length of this pole which in some cases impeded traffic.[10] Tavern-keepers would hang an ivy bush from the pole to indicate that they sold wine, and ale-sellers came to adopt the sign of the hoop, presumably a hoop of metal from an ale-barrel, to distinguish their houses. (There is no doubt, however, that the larger establishments, particularly inns, which offered food and accommodation also, sold both wine and ale, and there resulted a gradual blurring of the distinctions between the originally separate establishments.) Owners of ale-houses would not qualify for admission to the Brewers' Company, nor would they usually be able to afford the quarterage demanded.

Chapter Six

The Golden Age

THE sixteenth century was the heyday of the Livery Companies. In a period of comparative peace both at home and abroad, the country's trade increased steadily, and London, as the financial and trading capital, prospered. Leading merchants belonging to major crafts were often extremely wealthy, and a good portion of their wealth went to the Companies which continued to do much to maintain favourable conditions for their members' trade.

There was also some rivalry among the crafts, with Companies jockeying for positions of privilege and vying with each other in the provisions of well-appointed halls, regular feasts and other displays of wealth. Disputes over the exact order of precedence among Companies were finally settled when a decision of the Court of Aldermen in 1516 laid down the order, still observed today, by which the Brewers were ranked fourteenth among the City Companies.[1] The order seems to have been decided according to the relative importance of the crafts, and only partially depended on dates of incorporation. The Mercers' Company, who ranked first, were incorporated in 1393, after the Weavers and Fishmongers. The hard-fought dispute between the Skinners and Merchant Taylors as to which Company should have precedence over the other was resolved by the decision of 1516, which declared that these two Companies should alternate annually for precedence.

This ruling also finally established the leading 'Great Twelve' Companies[2] – those of the most important and wealthiest trades – and membership of one of these Companies became almost essential for anyone wishing to rise in civic government; the

Lord Mayor was chosen almost invariably from one of these Companies, and so it became an accepted practice that any member of a small, less significant Livery Company would, if desirous of obtaining some civic office, transfer membership to one of the leading Companies, regardless of the trade he actually followed. Such was the case with John Tate, a brewer, who later joined the Mercers' Company and became Lord Mayor in 1514. A few would still retain their membership of the lesser Company, as well as enrolling in one of the Great Twelve, but this could be a costly business, for there were fines payable on gaining the freedom of a Company and also quarterage was often heavy in order to provide funds for suitable upkeep of Companies' halls and various, often considerable, expenses considered necessary for the adequate support of the Company's public image and private satisfaction.

As mentioned above, however, wealthy merchants were only too happy to give support to their Livery Company in the form of money, property or possessions, and the foundations of the present wealth of many Companies were laid in the sixteenth century. Money for charity was also often entrusted to a Company by the will of a deceased member. An important factor in the general amassing of wealth by the Livery Companies at this time was the Reformation. The religious element in the make-up of the Companies, already examined, could have made them very vulnerable in the general purge and the commandeering by the Crown of Church property and monies, for most Companies had formerly been entrusted with money for the upkeep of chantries, and for masses and the conduct of a funeral of a deceased member. It was to every man a great matter that there should be money enough to give him a decent burial, and it was, as it had been among the early fraternities, still considered necessary for members of a Company to attend the funeral of a fellow member. Many Companies had their own pall to be used at members' funerals. The Brewers' Company is one of the few to still have a pall, and its magnificence, red velvet richly embroidered with gold thread, would have been in keeping with the pomp and ceremony of a Company funeral.[3]

With the Reformation, however, it became politic quietly to abandon any practices which were so fundamentally a part of

the old religion, and a wealthy man would no longer leave money
or property for the provision of masses for his soul. Money that
might have been used in such a way in the fifteenth century,
came in the sixteenth century to be employed for more general
charitable purposes, and Companies found themselves admini-
stering trusts for the establishment of schools, almshouses and
general poor relief. The aforementioned John Tate, brewer and
mercer, had his brewery, situated next to St Anthony's Hospital,
demolished so that the hospital could be enlarged and almshouses and a free school established. The growing wealth of
some City merchants meant that there was money available for
sizable endowments of this kind, and the Livery Companies,
now with a long-established tradition of charitable work, and
known and trusted by their members, were well suited to the
administration of these ventures.

Other repercussions of the Reformation were felt in the field
of education, previously in the hands of the clergy, who had
now either to abjure their faith or flee the country. At the same
time, men were becoming increasingly aware of the need for
education, and thus the founding of a school became a favourite
charitable objective. Two of the major charities administered
by the Brewers' Company and founded at this time are educa-
tional concerns. In 1595 Alderman Richard Platt, of the Old
Swan Brewery, obtained Letters Patent from the Queen to
found a school and almshouses at Aldenham in Hertfordshire.[4]
In 1599 he drew up his orders for the school and appointed the
Brewers as Governors. The orders he compiled are detailed,
for he said that 'nothinge well begonne can longe contynewe
in good order unles the same be directed and governed by good
ordynances lawes and statutes'. For the appointment of the
Master he required that

the Master of my Schoole be honeste religious of good conversac[. . .]on
well reported of learned in the toungs a Mr of Arts in degree if itt posseblie
maye be me in my lief tyme and after my deathe ever to be chosen and
admytted by my trustie and welbeloved ffriendes the Master Wardynes and
Assistantes of the Companye of Brewers of London for the tyme beinge att
a Court of Assistants to be kepte for the same Companye wherein twelve
or more of the Assistants shalbe assembled. To whose wysdome and discretion I comytt the government of this my saide schoole.

The Elizabethan 'Free Grammar School' at Aldenham. Drawn by the school surveyor before demolition in 1825, the engraving was made to order of the Governors in 1828. *Aldenham School*

Among the orders to be observed by the Master and the Usher, Platt demands 'that neyther the Maister nor Ussher shall gyve themselves to games nor hauntinge of Alehowses and Tavernes unbeseeminge places suche Persons as governe others leaste theire evill examples breede nott onlye descreditt to the Schoole but infection also to the Schoollers to whome I woulde have them patternes of vertue honestie and pyetie'.[5]

The school and also the almshouses are still flourishing, as is the Company's other school, founded in 1613 under the will of Dame Alice Owen. Dame Alice outlived three husbands, and two of these had been brewers. There is no evidence that she herself was a member of the Brewers' Company, though as a widow of a brewer she would have been eligible; but in her will she entrusted the government of almshouses and a school which she had recently established at Islington to her friends the

Watercolour of the original almshouses at Aldenham, by J. Buckler, 1832. At the end nearest the school is the chapel, a small room in which the Master said daily prayers. *Aldenham School*

Master and Wardens of the Company of Brewers of London. The income for the school was to come from a parcel of land known as the Ermitage Fields, and Dame Alice's will also required a further piece of land to be purchased to provide a salary for the Schoolmaster. The story behind the foundation of Dame Alice's school has become legendary; different versions vary as to the details, but David Davis, Headmaster of the school from 1750 to 1791, gave this account of it in a letter to the Master of Brewers' Company in 1773:

Lady Owen was a gentlewoman of very reputable birth and education, being the daughter of Wilkes, Esq., a Gentleman of great landed property in Islington. One morning Lady Owen (then Miss Wilkes) taking the benefit of an airing in the fields nearby or upon the very spot where her School and Almshouses now stand which was then, or part thereof, a Cow Layer, attended by her maid-servant, stopped by mere curiosity to milk a cow and in the very moment of stooping, an arrow from the cross-bow of a Gentleman taking his diversion with it according to the custom of the times, happened in its flight to be so critically directed as to strike and carry away with it the high-crowned hat she wore without doing any injury to her person; it is imagined had she unfortunately happened to be at this instant in an erect posture the arrow would certainly have proved fatal. Whereupon, the Lady, sensible for her singular delivery, declared should it please providence to bless her with the smiles of affluence, or an ample fortune, would gratefully perpetuate to posterity her sense of the Divine Assistance she had experienced by some Charitable Foundation.

The Brewers' Company was not the only Livery Company to be entrusted with administration of education charities, and this extension of Companies' charitable work was to be of major importance for the future. At the time, this side-effect of the Reformation made little change in Companies' daily business, which was still concerned mainly with matters pertaining to trade. The money and property which such trusts brought under the Companies' control did, however, help to increase their prestige.

Another side-effect of the Reformation was the discreet dropping of any earlier overt religious affiliations. New charters issued by Elizabeth incorporated Companies under the names of their trade, and references to patron saints were omitted. The Brewers were one of several Companies who also judged it advisable to apply for a new coat of arms. The Brewers had first been granted a coat of arms in 1468 and the heraldic description by William Hawkslowe, Clarenceux, runs: 'Asure thre barly sheves, gold bound of the same, a cheveron gawles in the chevron thre barels, silver garnyshed with sable.' These arms the Company had impaled with those of their patron, St Thomas à Becket, but at the time of the Reformation this public image of allegiance to a saint who had been so very outspoken in defence of the old Church was not considered politic. In 1544 the Company obtained a second grant of arms:

Gueles on a chevron engrailed silver thre kelderkyn sable hoped, golde between syx barly sheves in saultre of the same. Vpon the Helme on a terse silver and asur a demy morien in her proper couler uestid asur freted silver to here golde holding in either hande thre barly eres of the same manteled sable dobled silver. Motto, in God is all our trust.[6]

The Company's patron was not forgotten in this new grant of arms, but to the uninitiated the connection is far from obvious. It is in the 'demy morien', and is based on a legend concerning Becket's father, Gilbert, a London merchant, who when on a trading expedition had been taken prisoner by pirates off the North African coast. He had been helped to escape by a Moorish lady, who then followed him to London and later married him, becoming Thomas's stepmother. How much truth there is in such a tale is impossible to discover, but it is fact that after the death of his first wife, Gilbert Becket married a girl from the South of France. For the Brewers, however, the story provided the basis for proclaiming their patron in a style subtle enough to arouse no query from those anxious to do away with all links with the Roman Church.

But if the Livery Companies found it advisable to adapt themselves to the new scheme of things created by the Reformation, it seems also unlikely that the Tudor sovereigns would have thought to launch any attack against them on religious grounds, for the Companies were loyal supporters of the Crown, and in the course of the century provided large sums of money towards its expenses. At the time of the Armada all the City Companies subscribed to equip a force of 4,000 men for the defence of London. The chronicler Stow recorded that 100 of these were supplied by the Brewers' Company.[7] To alienate such a source of revenue would not have been wise.

The City, too, began to look to the Livery Companies for financial help. In 1521 the first loan was ordered to be raised from the Companies by Common Council, who required £1,000 for the purchase of corn to ensure the City's supplies. Another loan for the same purpose was raised in 1573, when the Brewers' Company were required to contribute £7 5s. od.[8] During Elizabeth's reign many Companies also sought new charters, for which payment had to be made to the Crown.

The Brewers received two charters from Elizabeth, one in 1560, and a second in 1579, which extended the jurisdiction of the Company to a two-mile radius outside the City. This was a matter of considerable satisfaction to the Brewers, as it now gave them the right to control the large number of brewers, particularly beer-brewers, who had set up business in Southwark,

Statue of Dame Alice Owen in bronze, alabaster and ebony, by George Frampton. *Collection Dame Alice Owen's School*

The old Grammar School of Lady Owen – a nineteenth-century watercolour of the first building. *Collection Dame Alice Owen's School*

hitherto beyond the Company's charter limits. And Southwark had become a very profitable suburb. For sixteenth-century Londoners it was the place to go to for entertainment and relaxation, much as the West End is today. Beyond the jurisdiction of the Lord Mayor, it was to Southwark the citizens went to watch bear-baiting, cock-fighting and, above all, the drama at the new theatres. The first theatre was built on Bankside in 1587 by the actor Philip Henslowe, and it was soon followed by others, the most famous being the Globe, headquarters of Shakespeare's Company.

In such an area there were obviously ample opportunities for the brewer to do business. Some of the entertainments actually took place in the courtyards of the larger inns, and the local taverns were certainly frequented by the actors. The playwright Christopher Marlowe was killed in a drunken brawl in South-

Charter granted by Elizabeth I to the Brewers' Company in 1579, extending its jurisdiction over Southwark. *Guildhall Library; photo, J. R. Freeman Ltd*

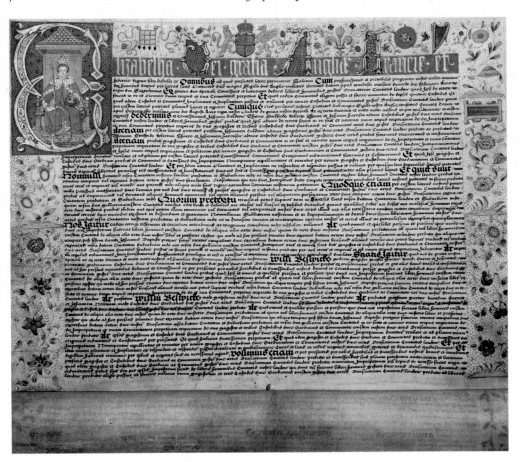

(*Above*) The Company pall. Company funerals were held until the Reformation.
The Museum of London; photo, Derrick Witty

(*Opposite*) The gateway to Brewers' Hall, Addle Street. A late Victorian watercolour.
Guildhall Library

Silver from the Company's collection: late seventeenth-century knife and fork with snake-skin case; George II snuffbox, coffee pots and tankard; George III teapot and rosebowl. *Photo, Derrick Witty*

wark, and there is a contemporary account of how Shakespeare and Ben Jonson would meet at the Mermaid Tavern.[9]

The opposition of the ale-brewers to the use of hops seems to have died out by the end of the sixteenth century, as more people began to acquire a taste for beer, and the Brewers too began to find advantages in the preservative value of hops, for ale had only a short life. This was undoubtedly of value to the large brewers who sold much of their beer wholesale to small retailers. As more brewers began to use hops, the old distinction between ale and beer was gradually dropped and beer became the more common drink.

For the extension of their charter limits the Brewers no doubt paid handsomely, but they could afford to. The increasing population of London brought an increase in the demand for beer and ale, and many brewers seem to have taken advantage of being the suppliers of such a necessary commodity to raise prices and make considerable profits. In 1551, after the Brewers had repeatedly ignored the Mayor's attempts to control prices, the Company was temporarily barred from the Common Council, and in the same year the first Surveyors of Beer were appointed by the Common Council. These officers, four in number, were originally required to inspect only beer, the standards of the ale-brewers being controlled by the City Aleconners, as well as by Wardens of the Brewers' Company; but five years later a further Act provided for the beer-brewers to come under the Brewers' Company. This was presumably a further attempt to control prices and also the quality of the brews, to ensure particularly that enough cheap, or single, beer was brewed. Profits on double beer, a strong brew, were much better than on single, so brewers tended to reduce the amount of single beer they produced and those who could not afford the higher price had to go without. Cheap beer was often of very poor quality, and the powers of search and in-spection vested in Wardens of the Company were not strictly prac-tised or it would not have been necessary for the Mayor to order on one occasion that fifty-two barrels of beer 'being neither fit for man's body nor to be converted into sawce shall have the heads of all the same beaten out, and the beer poured into the channells part in Cheapside, part in Cornhill, and part in Bishops-gate'.[10]

The opportunities of making greater profits and expanding business were taken up by the Brewers, as by other traders, at the expense of standards. Although the Companies still sought to maintain the quality of their crafts, the increased population made it more difficult to carry out surveys regularly and many leading merchants were more interested in the expansion of their own business to be too concerned to keep rigidly to an established standard. It was the growing pursuit of individual wealth rather than the common good that led to the gradual decline in the influence of the Livery Companies in City trade.

Chapter Seven

A Company in Decline

THE end of the Tudor monarchy was also the end of the golden
age of the Livery Companies. From the early years of the
seventeenth century there was a gradual but definite decline in
their power and influence as the leading institutions of City trade.
In the municipal government they continued to play a major
role; but the power of the Mayor and Aldermen over trading
matters was also to fall away with the growth of large businesses
in the eighteenth century.

One important cause of the Companies' decline was the
diminishing enthusiasm for membership. When the Livery
Companies were first formed a trader could greatly benefit from
belonging to one. They were concerned with promoting the
interests of their own trade and protecting their members from
outside competition; and by a united effort it had been possible
to gain rights and privileges which the individual small trader
could not otherwise have hoped to attain. But by the seventeenth
century these advantages were no longer so desirable when the
disadvantages were also considered.

The growing population and the spread of people to the
suburbs meant that the monopoly of trade which Companies
possessed became increasingly impossible to maintain in practice.
The rights of search and inspection were difficult to carry out in
the over-populated City, and in the suburbs the Companies
had no authority at all. In an attempt to reassert the Companies'
powers of control, the civic authorities recommended that their
charter limits should be extended so as to include most of the
suburbs. The Brewers' Company Charter issued by Charles I

in 1639 does in fact extend the limits to a four-mile radius, but it proved impossible in practice to enforce controls over such a wide area. It was quite feasible to practise a trade without having the trouble and expense involved in membership of a Livery Company. And membership of a Company was becoming expensive. As well as the upkeep of halls, feasts, livery gowns, etc., both the Crown and the City itself now made regular demands for financial help on the Companies and money requested for these 'forced loans' had to be found even if unwillingly.

Opposition grew noticeably under the heavy demands of Charles I. It is recorded that as early as 1604 the Wardens of the Brewers' Company were imprisoned in the Wood Street Compter for refusing to pay their contribution towards the expenses incurred by the City for a royal progress. The Company received new charters from James I and Charles I, not to acquire new powers, but so that the Crown could claim payment for granting them. Usually demands were met, either out of quarterage or from a special levy on members. Companies' expenses became so great that many small traders could not afford to belong, while wealthier members of the craft preferred to devote their time and money to forwarding their own business. It was the smaller Livery Companies that suffered most from this falling-off; it was still considered advantageous to belong to one of the prestigious Great Twelve, particularly if a person was ambitious. It had become customary for the Lord Mayor to be chosen from the Twelve and until the early seventeenth century Aldermen, too, were elected only from these Companies. Thus Alderman Isaac Pennington, a Member of Parliament for the City, was a well-known brewer in the 1640s, but he became a member of the Fishmongers' Company.[1]

A major money-raising scheme by James I involved the Livery Companies in Ireland. Keeping the Irish subjugated to the Crown had always been a problem for the monarchy, and James adopted the policy of dispossessing the natives of their land and settling Englishmen there to keep control. In 1610 James offered large tracts of land in Ulster to the twelve great Livery Companies for the sum of £60,000, thus establishing English landlords, albeit absentees, over a large area and at the same time acquiring some much needed money. Each of the

Great Twelve was to put up £5,000, and to help raise the money the minor companies were also permitted to take a share. Thus it was that the Brewers' Company contributed £700 towards the Ironmongers' sum and became a member of the Irish Society, which was set up to administer the Ulster plantation. Originally the whole plantation was under the control of the Governors and Assistants of the Irish Society, but in 1618 it was found practical to divide most of the lands between the individual Companies who had contributed to their purchase. The Iron-mongers' share was the Manor of the Lizard, and of this the Brewers became the owners of three separate parcels of land made up of the estates of Clacan, Edenbane, Trinaltenach, Cuil-bane, Tirkeeran, Drumbane, Carticlouchan and Magheramore.[2]

The Companies did not remain long in possession of the Irish estates however, for in 1637 Charles I demanded that they be surrendered to the Crown, in return for granting the City a new charter. As the charter gave no new benefits and Charles was faced with continued rebellion in Ireland, neither side seems to have profited by this, and in 1663 Charles II granted another charter to the Irish Society and the land again reverted to the Companies.

The Companies were traditional supporters of the Crown, but it is not surprising to find that enthusiasm waned with the continuous demands for financial help made by James and Charles I. Although when Charles made a progress through the City in 1641 the Livery Companies lined the streets in loyal support, when civil war broke out the following year the liverymen did not rally to the royalist cause, and as there was also strong Puritan support among the middle classes of London, particularly in the suburbs, the City fell to Cromwell without a battle.

It is curious to find that, in spite of Puritan opposition to drink and the drunkenness which was becoming an increasing problem in London, many brewers were leading supporters of the new religion. Isaac Pennington, mentioned above, who was a leading brewer in the City, had also a reputation as a staunch Puritan and his wife, daughter of another brewer, frequently entertained leading Puritan clergy at their inn at Whitefriars. Southwark, refuge of brewers aiming to escape their Company's governance, was a stronghold of Puritanism; but it seems that support for

The charter of Charles I, 1639. *Guildhall Library*

it was to be found also within the Brewers' Company. In the 1640s a royalist pamphleteer, Taylor, attempted to bring discredit to a number of men known to advocate religious and political reforms, among whom he names Quatermaine, a clerk in the Brewers' Company.

But objections to drunkenness on religious grounds did not interfere with business where the Brewers were concerned, and brewing was a growing industry in the seventeenth century. Drunkenness, too, however was a growing problem. In 1614 the then Lord Mayor, 'finding the gaols pestered with prisoners,

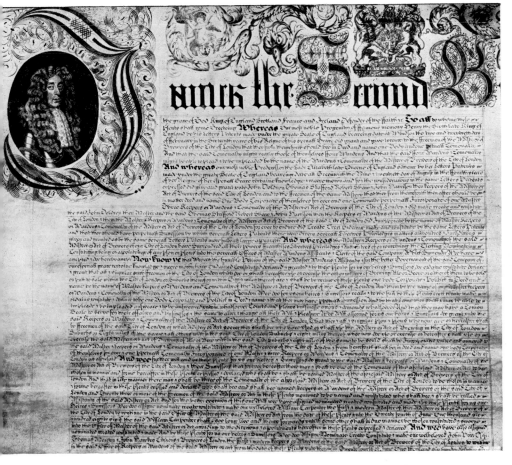

James II's charter, dated 18 March 1684/5. *Guildhall Library*

and their bane to take root and beginning at ale-houses and much
mischief to be there plotted with great waste of corn in brewing
headstrong beer, many consuming all their time and means in
sucking that sweet poison',[3] attempted to restrict the number of
ale-houses in the City, which then numbered over 1,600. Brewers
were also accused of deliberately brewing ale stronger than the
standard laid down by the Assize, thus promoting drunkenness.
The first beer duty was introduced in 1643 to raise money, but
it was also aimed at restricting the production of strong beer
by levying a considerably higher duty on the more powerful

brews. One London brewer in 1647 published a vindication of strong beer:

Of hops and malt, our native commodities (and therefore the more agreable to the constitutions of our native inhabitants), may be made such strong beer (being well boiled and hopped, and kept its full time) as that it may serve instead of Sack . . . such good strong beer as shall be most cherishing to poor labouring people, without which they cannot well subsist; their food being for the most part of such things as afford little or bad nourishment, nay, sometimes dangerous, and would infect them with many sicknesses and diseases, were they not preserved (as with an antidote) with good beer, whose virtues and effectual operations, by help of the hop well boiled in it, are more powerful to expel poisonous infections than is yet publicly known or taken notice of.[4]

The medicinal qualities must be dubious, but beer was still the main drink for all men, and sales were obviously high enough for most brewers not to be unduly troubled by the heavier duty imposed on strong beers. Output and profits continued to increase until towards the end of the seventeenth century, when various factors combined to result in a perceptible cutback.

One factor was an increase in the Excise Duty. This was first levied on beer by Cromwell, but was retained after the Restoration as a most useful source of revenue. In 1692 this duty was increased to 5s. a barrel, a rate which considerably increased the cost of beer for brewer and consumer. Another, and more important, cause for the reduced quantities of beer produced, was the introduction and rapid increase in popularity of other drinks. Tea was first imported into England in 1666 and, although extremely expensive at first, it proved popular with those who could afford it. Coffee was also introduced, and this was less expensive. The first London coffee-house was opened in 1652, and coffee and chocolate became so popular that in 1673 the Brewers petitioned Parliament to prohibit the sale of these beverages as they much reduced the sale of beer.

Tea and coffee, however, were not intoxicating, but gin was, and in the late seventeenth century this was beer's most serious rival. The Brewers' Company, to offset the growing popularity of gin, obtained permission from Charles II for brewers also to distil spirits, but they continued to campaign against the sale of gin which was relatively cheap and so particularly popular with those who had little money to get drunk on. It was also usually on sale at coffee-houses which meant customers did not need to visit the ale-house, the accepted outlet for the sale of beer. But the Brewers could no longer be blamed for the high incidence of drunkenness; indeed, the critics of the expanding gin trade were often eager to point out the virtues of the native and less noxious beer. In 1736 Parliament passed the Gin Act in an attempt to curb the sale of spirits in small quantities. The act required retailers of spirits to obtain a licence at the cost of £50 and a duty of 20s. per gallon was raised on the distilling of spirits. Judging by the number of fines levied as a result of the infringement of the law and the continued high rate of drunkenness among all classes, the Act does not seem to have been very effective!

These changes in the nation's drinking habits and the duty payable on brewing beer (a malt tax, and later a tax on hops, had been introduced, in addition to the Excise Duty, mentioned above) combined to check the steady growth of the brewing industry at the end of the seventeenth century and in the early eighteenth century.

The fortunes of the Brewers' Company reflected those of the industry. The first half of the seventeenth century had seen some falling-off in the power of the Livery Companies as the controllers of the City's trade, but it was the Great Fire of 1666 that really brought to an end all effective exercise of the extensive rights they had won. The fire is believed to have destroyed forty-four livery halls, among them the old Brewers' Hall in Addle Street, which Stow's 1603 *Survey of London* described as 'a fayre house'. Some of the smaller Companies could not afford to rebuild their halls, some adopted the habit of renting the hall of one of the larger Companies to conduct their business. From 1667 the Brewers used the Cooks' Hall for their affairs, but they decided to maintain their status and build a new hall on the site of the old.

The Company had great difficulty in raising the money for the new hall. A subscription of £5 was required from every member; those who declined to pay were fined. A few members promised materials for the work; one liveryman, a Mr Girl, offered 50,000 bricks! More money was got from pawning the

Interior of an ale-house *circa* 1628. The woodcut, illustrating a ballad, is in the British Museum. *Radio Times Hulton Picture Library*

Company's plate and pictures which had been saved from the fire and which they could not later afford to redeem.[5] Yet other contributions came from newly admitted freemen, who thus avoided paying the usual fine on admission. On 16 March 1670 a Mr Whiteing and Mr Aldridge appeared before the Company's Court to put forward a suggested design for the new building, and in May two tenders for the work were received from Mr Ball for £3,443, and from Captain Caine for £3,523. The bargaining then began. To start with, both builders were asked if they would allow £3,000 for the old materials: an audacious request, which both refused. They were then asked by how much they would be willing to cut their price, and after much wrangling Captain Caine was given the contract for £3,300.

When it was finally completed in 1673 the total cost of the new hall amounted to £5,827 16s. 8d. Captain Caine was admitted as a member of the Company in recognition of 'his care and diligence in building the Hall'. There are many pictures and descriptions of the hall to testify to this diligence. One of its main features was the courtroom, the wainscotting for which was

provided by Sir Samuel Starling, Alderman and Lord Mayor
in 1670, and Master of the Company in 1661. Starling was a
well-known figure in the City, but with the reputation of being
a hard businessman. An entry in Samuel Pepys's diary made at
the time of the Great Fire states that 'Alderman Starling, a very
rich man, without children, the fire at next door to him in our
lane, after our men had saved his house, did give 2s. 6d. among
thirty of them, and did quarrel with some that would remove the
rubbish out of the way of the fire, saying that they came to steal.'[6]

By the time the hall was finished, however, the Company had
little money and a dwindling membership. Most of the Livery
Companies faced the same problems. Although much of the
City had been rebuilt, many who had had to move out of the
City after the fire had settled in the suburbs and were now
reluctant to return. The City authorities and the Companies
united in an effort to encourage people to take up residence within the City again. It was agreed in 1673 that for a period of one
year all who wished to come to the City, provided they were
given the approval of the Court of Aldermen, should be granted
the freedom of the City without the usual payment of a fine, and
that they should then be made free of any Livery Company
which would accept them, also without a fine. This measure did
increase the number of applicants for livery membership but
the Companies still needed funds to pay their debts after rebuilding their halls, and the money could only be raised from
members, so despite free admission membership had become
more expensive than ever.

The Brewers' Company records show a considerable number
of admissions to the freedom at this time of men who were not
brewers at all. In November 1675, for example, Samuel Withers,
a shoemaker, was made free of the Company. It is clear that in
order to boost membership and funds the Brewers, as other
Companies, had ceased to require only those of their own trade
as freemen. There also seems to have been an increasing tendency
for liverymen, if they were ambitious and could afford it, to be
free of more than one Company. In January 1736 George Peys
is recorded as having the freedom of the Brewers' Company
and beside the entry, the comment 'is also of the Sadlers' Company and has served Master of that Company'.

Samuel Whitbread, by Joshua Reynolds. *Courtesy of Whitbread and Co. Ltd*

Meanwhile effective control of their trade was becoming increasingly difficult for all Companies. The expansion of industry in the suburbs was accelerated after the Great Fire sent many former City dwellers to settle elsewhere. New attempts were made to bring all the suburbs under the Companies' control by further extending their charter limits. In 1685 the Brewers received their eighth, and last, charter from James II, which extended their powers over all brewers within an eight-mile radius of the City, all of whom were required to become members of the Company; but in practice many still refused to join. Thus from the end of the seventeenth century the part played by the Livery Companies in trade affairs diminished rapidly, all effective control passing into the hands of the big businessmen with capital who were beginning to establish industries on a large scale. When the Brewers' Company drew up its Constitutions, Orders, Rules and Ordinances in 1739, although these rehearsed the charter provisions for compulsory membership and reaffirmed the Company's rights to search and exact penalties, they could not effectively be put into practice. A further attempt was made in 1753 to compel all City brewers to take up freedom of the Company, and legal advice was sought from several counsels as to whether the charter requirements could be enforced by law, but the decision went against the Company. The committee set up to inquire into the matter reported to the Court 'that Counsel were unanimous in their opinions that we could not justify the search or oblige non-freemen of the Company to pay Quarterage or compel persons occupying the trade of a Brewer within 4 miles of the City of London to take up the freedom of your Company notwithstanding the Charter and Bye-Laws have delegated such power to the Company; for that your Charter and Bye-Laws can only bind your own members by law'.[7]

The Brewers' Company records for the eighteenth century reflect the decline of its power within the trade. The Court of Assistants still met regularly, but little of commercial importance was discussed. An agenda for a Court meeting in 1793 declared the business for the morning to be a report on the Irish lands, the election of a new Middle Warden and two liverymen, an explanation why a Mr Thomas Collier refused to serve as Steward the previous year and the appointment of a new Master at Aldenham – not a meeting which would be likely to interest busy men intent on building up their own businesses.

It is noticeable that the leading brewers of the period, although they were freemen of the Company, took little interest in its affairs and wherever possible avoided taking office, which could make demands on their time and money that they were unwilling to spend away from their own businesses. Some preferred to be fined rather than take office or, if elected, would pay fines rather than attend frequent meetings. Henry Thrale, who inherited the Anchor Brewery in Southwark from his father in 1759, was fined for his non-attendance as Renter Warden in 1770, and even when he became Master in 1773 he repeatedly failed to attend when required.[8] Samuel Whitbread, who had joined the Company as an apprentice in 1736 (he was bound to the then Master of the Company, John Wightman, for £300), was an active member until his own brewery began to expand and in 1757 he resigned his place on the Court due to the increasing demands of his own affairs.

The Company had not, however, ceased to have any function in the trade. Anyone wishing to become a master brewer still had to serve his seven years' apprenticeship, bound to a recognized master, and become a freeman. All apprenticeships were registered with the Company. The Company also provided a useful organ for bringing members of the brewing trade together for a common cause. Under the auspices of the Company, brewers of all ranks could conveniently unite, to bring pressure on national or municipal government in matters of concern to the trade as a whole. In this way, the Company supported a number of petitions to Parliament aimed at improving the Brewers' lot. In 1726 Parliament was asked to tax all private brewing which cut the sales of the commercial brewer. The same year the Company petitioned on behalf of all victualling trades for the abolition of the Pot Act, and continued pressure resulted in this Act eventually being repealed in 1742. In 1772, after a failure of the hop harvest, the Company sought permission for brewers to import Flemish hops.

To get these petitions heard in high quarters, however, the Company relied increasingly on the interest of the major brewers

Benjamin Truman, by Thomas Gainsborough. *Courtesy of Watney, Mann and Truman Breweries Ltd*

like Thrale who were already Members of Parliament and men of influence. When it prepared the 1772 petition, the Court specifically requested that Samuel Whitbread, Henry Thrale and Robert Calvert aid their negotiations with Parliament. It was an acknowledgement that these men had developed their business to such an extent that they did not need the support and protection offered by the Brewers' Company, but rather that the Company looked to them to promote the interests of its members in trade matters.

Whitbread and Thrale had before the end of the eighteenth century become large-scale wholesalers of beer and they, and men such as Benjamin Truman and John Watney, were laying the foundations of the great national brewery companies of the twentieth century. At this time when brewing was becoming more scientific the equipment needed for a big brewery was expensive. But for those who could afford it, this new machinery could enable large quantities of beer to be brewed at one time with a saving of manpower and cost. Those with the capital to invest in such equipment had the prospect of considerable returns, and in the recently invented porter they had a product ideal for mass production.

Porter was a brew which particularly lent itself to production and sale on a large scale. It was invented by an East End brewer named Harwood in 1722. Before its introduction, the usual brews on sale at an ale-house would be a strong ale, a beer which was weaker, and 'tuppenny ale' of a higher quality. Customers, however, usually drank a combination of these, and Harwood's brew was a liquor similar in taste to this mixture, but which could be more easily served, being drawn from just one barrel instead of two or three. The new brew quickly became popular, and Harwood called it 'porter' after his customers, most of whom were porters and carters. It was 'porter' that the large brewers found most profitable to produce, and to retail through their own ale-houses.[9]

As the small brewers and ale-house keepers found it increasingly hard to compete with the prices of the wholesalers, they were encouraged to become retailers for the bigger breweries, and thus gain a measure of security and protection. This was the beginning of the tied-house system. The extension

Sketch from the Brewers Scrapbook

of the licensing laws also gave a boost to this system. It was 1753 when the first law to introduce a system of annual licences for all beer and spirit retailers was passed; ten years later this Act was extended to require all licensees to give a guarantee that their premises were of a size big enough to accommodate customers. These regulations were not at first by any means strictly enforced, but the large wholesalers found that small traders could be encouraged to become retailers of their brews by offering to bring old premises up to the standard required for a licence.

Thus by the end of the eighteenth century the brewing trade was divided between the large and rapidly expanding whosesale breweries and the smaller businesses, many of which were being bought up by the big breweries. The Brewers' Company had ceased to be a powerful or truly representative body within the trade, for the small traders were often unable to afford to belong while the leading brewers had no need of the Company's support. Brewers' Hall, however, did provide a convenient meeting place for the Brewers, and also a place to dine well, for the traditionally lavish dinners had continued through the years, perhaps as an enticement to reluctant members to attend. The Company's Scrapbook contains a number of menus and bills for these dinners and other entertainments at this time. The bill for the election dinner in 1792 is a typical one:

6 Dishes of Fish	£6 6s. od.
6 Chickens	14s. od.
6 Capons	18s. od.
2 Hams	£1 18s. od.
5 Haunches of Venison	£15 os. od.
1 Neck	18s. od.
4 Venison Pasties	£2 2s. od.
2 Geese	15s. od.
4 Ducks	12s. od.
9 Dishes of Greens and Cauliflower	9s. od.
8 Tarts	£2 os. od.
8 Dishes of French Beans	12s. od.
Lobster, Shrimp, Anchovy Sauce, Plain, Butter & Gravy	£1 16s. od.
2 Legs Mutton Cooked	15s. od.
Coals & Wood	£1 10s. od.
Currant Jelly	15s. od.
Use of Queens Ware	£1 15s. od.
Salt, Butter	5s. 6d.
2 Quartern Loaves	1s. 2d.
	£41 11s. 8d.[10]

The cost of such dinners, however, must have been heavy on the Company's funds, for there are also indications that attempts were made to curb this expenditure. A bill for a meal from 1760 has a note written on the bottom: 'Our dinner came to rather too much last time',[11] and in 1784 there was a meeting at the Amsterdam Coffee House of 'the Committee appointed to regulate the Company's expenses in the Entertainment', at which the following decisions were taken:

(1) That it is their opinion that the Audit Dinner may be for the present laid aside and that a Committee of the whole Court may be appointed to audit the accounts for which they shall be allowed Court money as usual.

(2) That it is the opinion of your Committee that for the future your Cook lay a bill of fare before the Court on the Court day preceding every Lord Mayor's Day and Election Day and that an agreement be made with him for the dinner he is to provide for each day the expenses whereof shall not exceed £26.

(3) That it is the opinion of the Committee that no person without leave of the Master, Wardens or Warden shall be admitted to dine in the Hall on Lord Mayor's Day or Election Day except the Livery.

Resolved also that it is their opinion that no French wine, old hock or punch shall be drank at the Company's expense at any of their entertainments.[12]

The Brewers' Scrapbook is a fascinating 800-page volume of bills, menus, agendas, letters, notes and memoranda of all kinds, mostly from the seventeenth, eighteenth and nineteenth centuries, though a few are of an earlier date. These are all stuck quite haphazardly into the large leather-bound book, many pages of which are decorated with drawings and sketches of faces. The book was, it has been assumed, compiled by the Clerk in the late nineteenth century, and it has been suggested that the pencil sketches were of the then members of Court. It provides an accurate picture of the Company's daily concerns at this time, an invaluable supplement to the Minute Books, which record only briefly the main items of business.

Both Minutes and Scrapbook bear out the Company's declining involvement in the commercial affairs of its members, and charitable work comes to figure more prominently. The Company was now the trustee of three schools, Aldenham, Dame Alice Owen's and James Hickson's School, the latter having been established in 1686 under the will of Alderman James Hickson at All Hallows, Barking, and endowed by the Manor of Williotts. Hickson also left money for almshouses to be built at South Mimms, Hertfordshire, for which the Company was also responsible. Each school and almshouse received an annual visitation from the Court, which examined the pupils' progress and assessed the good behaviour of the almswomen.

The tasks to be carried out at a visitation were not onerous. In 1737 members of the Court making the visitation to Owen's School and almshouses were bidden to inquire into the following matters:

If the Master hath absented himself from the School above ten days together during the last year without the Governors' leave.

If the Scholars are duly registered.

If any of the Scholars have absented themselves from the School above seven days together without the Master's leave.

If Prayers are duly read in the School twice every day.

If the Scholars keep their hands and faces clean and their Heads combed and their garments clean.

If Prayers are duly read to the poor twice every day and whether they attend at such prayers.

If any of them have absented themselves from their houses above three nights during the last year without leave of the Custos.

If they keep good hours and are not out of their houses after 7 o'clock in the Winter and 9 in the Summer, and if they keep the yard before their Almshouses neat and clean.

If they harbour any strangers or diseased persons in their houses.

If any of them is a Drunkard, Blasphemer, of dissolute or disorderly life or a wilful neglector of the Founder's Statutes.[13]

The Court obviously took these duties seriously, however. There are several instances of masters at Aldenham being reprimanded for their pupils' lack of progress.

Richard Platt's will gave members of the Company the right to have their sons educated at Aldenham at reduced fees. A grateful pupil in 1765 wrote to thank the Company for his education:

Gentlemen –

Permit me to return you my sincere thanks for the good Education I have had the opportunity of receiving under your Patronage; and give me leave to assure you that I will apply the advantages of it in such a manner, as shall best answer your earnest endeavours to establish the credit of the Schools, and be most correspondent to the intentions of its pious founder.[14]

The administration of the schools and upkeep of the buildings came to be a major part of the Company's business. There was also the upkeep of three sets of almshouses, Platt, Owen and Hickson, and the control of other charities, such as that established by Robert Hurst, who left money to provide clothes and

Interior of an ale-house *circa* 1740. *Radio Times Hulton Picture Library*

religious instructions for poor children in the parish of St Giles, Cripplegate. This work, together with the collection of rents from the Company's property in Islington, Williotts and South Mimms and maintenance of the hall itself, tended to replace matters of trade concern as the Company's main business. In 1795 serious direct participation in trade affairs finally passed from the Court to the newly formed Committee of Porter Brewers. To this all the leading brewers belonged and it was independent of the Company. Meetings, however, were held at Brewers' Hall, and the Committee employed the Company's Clerk to work for them at an additional salary. It is quite possible that it was the convenience of the hall as a meeting place both for work and pleasure that persuaded many of the large brewers to maintain their links with the Company at a time when other businessmen were beginning to neglect their Livery Companies.

Chapter Eight

Victorian Revival

THE *modus vivendi* evolved by the members of the Brewers' Company by the beginning of the nineteenth century proved remarkably successful, and the fundamental pattern has survived to the present day. The Company itself had become primarily an administrator of charitable trusts, in particular the Platt, Owen and Hickson foundations. The Court records reveal that matters other than domestic ones were seldom discussed at meetings; a typical nineteenth-century Court agenda is this one for July 1858:

To read and confirm the minutes of Court held on Friday 11th June last.

To report the examination of Alderman Richard Platt's Schools at Aldenham on 18th of the same month.

To elect an Exhibitioner to the University.

To report the election at Aldenham from nine candidates of Sarah Norris, Widow, aged 76 years to the Almshouse vacant by the death of Mrs Eliza Ellwood aged 80 years.

Letter from Mr John Brown Dutton as to his Head Monitor.

Rain-water tank at Medburn Farm.

To report the result of the trial at the Old Bailey of John Henry Grossmith for an assault upon the Rev. Edward John May.

Application from Mr Stokeham Huthwaite for assistance from Mr Whitbread's Great Barford Fund.

Application from Miss Martin, the daughter of a late Almswoman at Islington.

To report the death of Sir Edward North Buxton, Bart., late an Assistant.

To report the death of Mrs Sarah Sale late a Clerkenwell inmate of Lady Owen's Almshouses.

To report as to the Dean and Chapter of Saint Paul's proceeding in the Sale of the reversion of Estates held of them upon renewable leases.

Application for admission to the Freedom by Redemption from Mr Henry Laribond of Bridgwater, Solicitor.[1]

But through the Committee of Porter Brewers the Company also remained closely involved in the brewing trade. The main concern of the Committee was price regulation. Although the major brewers were competing with each other for wholesale and retail trade, they all saw the advantages of co-operation over price maintenance. The steady growth of the big breweries through the nineteenth century was encouraged by increased mechanization which required considerable capital investment, beyond the means of the small brewer. Domestic brewing also declined, for the increased use of tea and coffee meant that the time spent brewing beer purely for home consumption was no longer worth while. The small brewer was less and less able to compete with the prices of the large-scale brewery with many wholesale and retail outlets. This was true of the country as a whole at this time; but the trend was particularly marked in the large towns, where there was plenty of cheap labour and no transport problems.

As the minor breweries went out of business and were taken over by the large progressive companies, so the membership of the Brewers' Company also underwent a gradual change. In the early years of the nineteenth century the Company and its affairs still did not attract the major brewers; membership decreased and non-brewers were admitted on payment of the statutory fine (£1 according to the 1739 Bye-laws). There were always a number of up-and-coming men willing to buy themselves the City's freedom in this way, and the right of freemen of the Brewers' Company to have their sons educated at Aldenham was an attraction to some. Only six Courts a year were held in the 1830s, and all trade matters were discussed by the Committee of Porter Brewers. By the 1880s, however, things had changed; the small brewers were fast disappearing from the trade and the big businessmen were dominating the membership. The practice of electing members as representatives of their companies began, and a list of 1881, which gives the then current allocation of representatives to each company, shows membership was already confined to a very small number of major companies:

> Truman Hanbury and Buxton – 4
> Barclay Perkins – 6
> Charrington – 3
> Mann Crossman and Paulin – 2
> Young Bainbridge – 1
> Combe – 4
> Whitbread – 3
> Reid – 2
> Hoare – 1
> Courage – 1
> Watney – 2[2]

Brewers' Hall, the meeting place for the Committee of Porter Brewers, proved a pleasant and convenient venue for the London brewers to meet formally and informally for the discussion and resolution of common problems, and they no longer regarded livery affairs as trivial concerns beside their own businesses. By tacit consent, the Company did not continue trying to extend its membership as many other Companies did; rather, it was content to concentrate on recruiting and retaining the interest of the London brewers, for whose benefit the Company had originally been founded. Trade matters were again reported at Court meetings (though policy matters were usually dealt with in detail in Committee) and the election of members as representatives of their breweries, noted above, is an indication of the Company's determination to retain its trade allegiance.

When the Company revised its 1739 Ordinances in 1857 the rules for membership were reaffirmed. All members had to be brewers, brewing within the charter limits. The strict application of this rule and disappearance of all but a few of the small breweries around the City meant that membership was limited to a comparatively small number of men. But it also meant that there were few apprentices; all members were master brewers. An acknowledgement of this was made in 1885 when it was decided to elect members in future to the freedom, the livery and the Court at one and the same time. The Company had opted for

The Dame Alice Owen Boys' School in 1881. Watercolour by G. G. Woodward. *Collection Dame Alice Owen's School*

a small but select membership in its endeavour to survive not only as an administrator of charities but also as an active trade organization. In following this course the Brewers differed from the majority of City Companies, many of which, in an effort to maintain their positions, had opened their doors to applicants in widely differing professions, who had, perhaps, only a tenuous connection with the Company's own trade.[3] In several instances Companies no longer had a trade to represent; and the criticism sometimes levelled at Livery Companies for being no more than glorified City gentlemen's clubs had its foundation in changes brought about in their membership in the mid-Victorian period.

There was much to attract the Victorian businessmen in the livery world, and in many cases Companies prospered as they had not done for two centuries. One main reason for the revitalization was the great wealth which many Companies found themselves controlling as the result of the Victorian property boom. Many of the charities entrusted to Livery Companies in former years had been endowed with land and property; it was usually only minor bequests which relied solely on monetary endowment. In other cases, property had been left directly to Companies by past members. In the mid-nineteenth century such property greatly increased in value, particularly land in or adjacent to London, which was needed to provide housing for the City's rapidly expanding population. The expansion of industry and commerce attracted more people to the big cities, and new discoveries in medicine and science meant a greater life expectancy. Both factors increased the demand for housing in and around all large towns, and in particular London, then the acknowledged financial capital of Europe.

As a result of the great increase in the value of their property, many Livery Companies became unexpectedly wealthy, and in an age which respected wealth, economically astute businessmen found membership of a Company with money to spend and invest more attractive than belonging to a Company with no money. Also, with more people crowding into the cities, and the development of more highly mechanized industries backed by considerable capital, the disparity between rich and poor became more than ever marked. Many public-spirited Victorians were anxious to alleviate the sufferings of the poor, and many others were at least keen to be seen publicly to be doing something for charity. The Livery Companies, already trustees for many old-established charities, gave the City gentleman an outlet for his philanthropic tendencies without demanding much time or money from him; and at the same time he could enjoy the other advantages offered by the Company. Livery Companies were not guilty of the gross misappropriations of charitable funds which took place in Victorian England, and which were exposed by such socially conscious novelists as Charles Dickens and Charlotte Brontë, but it was not unusual for a profitable charity to provide the funds for a good dinner for the trustees until the Charity Commissioners exerted some stringent controls over these funds.

The Brewers were one of the Companies to benefit most by the increased value of property. The Livery Commission report of 1885 noted that, apart from the Great Twelve, the Brewers were the wealthiest of the minor companies, with an income in 1884 of £18,640.[4] Of this £15,482 was trust income, and most of this came from rents from the development of the Islington estate which Dame Alice Owen had provided as an endowment for her charity. What was once open fields now became an area of closely built residential properties, and the income from rents soared. Most of the building was completed in the 1880s; in the new development the old almshouses disappeared, and instead of rebuilding, elected almswomen were given an allowance of 12s. per week. The original school had been rebuilt in 1840, and further additions were made in the 1880s and 1890s.[5] Under the headmastership of James Easterbrook (1881–1909) the school gained the highest reputation, with every year bringing an outstanding list of examination successes and university awards. For over ten years Owen's School headed the list in the number of honours gained in the Cambridge local examinations. Then, in 1886, some of the new income was used to found Dame Alice Owen's Girls' School to help fulfil the demand for more education for women. The charity having been founded by a woman, it was doubtless thought fitting that money from it should be used to further female education, and in 1875 money from the Owen foundation was contributed to the North London Collegiate School founded twenty-five years earlier by the renowned Miss Buss.

The Platt Trust, not having comparable land endowments, did not incur the benefit of a similar substantial increase in income. The Charity Commissioners' report on the Aldenham School made in 1817 showed that the income was growing, mainly from the leasing of lands at St Pancras. The Commission criticized the Company for not putting this income to use to benefit the school, at that time short of pupils and housed in unsatisfactory buildings. In 1825 the Company decided to rebuild the school and advertise for more pupils. The 1833 prospectus, a copy of which is included in the Company's Scrapbook, is amusing and illuminating reading:

The School is situated in a very healthy and beautiful part of Hertfordshire, about 13 miles from London. It was founded by virtue of a Charter granted by Queen Elizabeth; and was rebuilt in the year 1825 by the Worshipful Company of Brewers, with very superior accommodation for Boarders.

An Annual Examination takes place at Midsummer, and Prizes are adjudged by the Worshipful Company of Brewers, to those who have made the greatest proficiency in their studies.

The System of Education comprises the Latin and Greek Languages, English Reading, Grammar and Composition; Writing and Arithmetic; the various branches of Mathematics; History, Geography, the Use of Globes, etc.

Each Pupil will have a separate bed.

The Terms for Board and Tuition, for Boys under fourteen years of age, are fifty guineas per annum.

For Boys above the age of fourteen years, sixty guineas.

For Boys who dine with the Master's family, and receive private lessons, eighty guineas.

Gentlemen who are preparing for Degrees or Holy Orders, will be received as Private pupils, at one hundred and twenty guineas per annum.

French, Dancing, Drawing, etc., will be taught by approved Masters, upon the usual terms.

No extra charge will be made beyond those for Books, Washing and Medical Attendance, if necessary.

Each Boy will be expected to provide himself with a silver spoon, two pairs of sheets and six towels.

A quarter's notice will be required, previous to the removal of a pupil.[6]

After the reorganization the school prospered, but the income did not continue to increase as the Charity Commissioners had expected. In 1881 the Brewers' Company gave a loan of £2,500 to the school to finance additional building. The Platt Alms-houses were rebuilt in 1862, under a scheme for the administration of the Platt Trust agreed between the Charity Commissioners and the Brewers' Company. The old almshouses had stood beside the school, but in order to allow more space for the school the almshouses were rebuilt a short distance away at Delrow, together with a new elementary school to replace the former Aldenham 'Lower School'.

The Company itself benefited directly from some property deals. The land where the old barge house had stood at Hammersmith was let in 1847;[7] in 1873 a property known as the Moor Lane Estate, bequeathed to the Company by Robert Horne, was sold to the new Metropolitan Railway Company at a good profit. In 1860 the Company was able to afford £2,496 to purchase the freehold of the land in Addle Street where the hall stood,

Aldenham School, showing the largely nineteenth-century additions

and which had, since the first hall was built, been leased from Dean and Chapter of St Paul's. Extensive repairs to the hall were also undertaken at a cost of £2,417 8s. 2d. An end wall of the hall which had become dangerous was entirely rebuilt, and the old Clerk's house was finally pulled down. Two houses were built on part of the land and let as offices and dwellings.

It is not surprising that with control of what had grown to be a large income, the Company felt free to enjoy some of the wealth. Four dinners a year were held regularly in the 1870s and 1880s, the election dinner, the audit dinner and the Owen and Hickson visitation dinners. The latter two were certainly paid for out of trust income, and all, judging by the bills, were lavish. The Company's Memorandum Book notes fourteen toasts which were customarily drunk on these occasions, and bills totalling over £500 annually for food for the dinners were usual. This does not seem much today, but it provided four dinners in the grand style for the Court of hundred years ago. Entertainment between courses was also provided, usually musical; at the election dinner of 1884 the songs included the following 'Brewers' Glee':

> 'Tis merry, 'tis merry in Brewers' Hall,
>   While the welcome cup goes round,
> When assembled here at the Master's call,
>   Good humour and mirth abound.
>
> For here, in years that have long since past,
>   The tie of fellowship bound us,
> And here old Time, as he journeys along,
>   In harmony still has found us.
>
> Our flowing cups to the Master's health,
>   Around shall cheerily pass,
> The Song and the Glee, to enliven our board,
>   Shall join with the circling glass.

Chorus –
> Then fill the glass to our standing toast,
>   No divisions our union shall sever,
> May the Brewers' Company, root and branch,
>   In prosperity flourish for ever.[8]

This period of extravagance, however, had come to an end by the end of the century. The Charity Commissioners had already tightened their control over trust accounts to ensure that money was being spent only in accordance with the terms of the trust. In 1882 the City Livery Commission was set up to look into all facets of the City's Companies and to report on their function now that they were no longer effective trade organizations. Some Companies had ceased to have any links with their trades; others had no trade still existing: many were involved in the charities they governed, but a few had become little more than superior dining clubs. Yet the Companies were still a major part of City life; freedom of the City was only obtainable through a Company, the government of the City was still in the hands of liverymen, and the parliamentary franchise was also restricted to freemen, a right confirmed as late as 1832 by the parliamentary Reform Act.

The Livery Commission's report appeared in 1884 and the Companies found themselves required to make an effort to regain some of the respect they had lost. In particular, care was to be taken to ensure that trust income was used only for charitable purposes, and a portion of the Companies' own income was to be devoted to purposes 'of acknowledged public utility'.[9] Freedom was still to be gained only through livery membership, but the right to elect the City's Members of Parliament was open to all householders, as indeed it already was in the rest of the country.

The Commission reported 'very favourably' on the conduct of the Brewers' Company, but it meant that the costly visitation dinners could no longer be financed from trust income. In the 1890s the election and audit dinners also began to lapse through lack of money. The cost of the Boer War both in men and money began to affect the whole country. There was a general tightening of belts, and the reports of the horrifying conditions at the front produced an atmosphere in which luxurious self-indulgence was regarded as unpatriotic. By the turn of the century the Brewers had almost abandoned their dinners, and instead concentrated on work for charities and for the trade.

Chapter Nine

New Roles for Old

IT may seem astonishing to many people that such institutions as the City Livery Companies should still survive and continue to take an active part in the City's life in the middle of the twentieth century. Not only have the old Companies adapted their constitutions and traditions to the needs of today's industrialized society, but new crafts have established their own Livery Companies. The Guild of Air Pilots and Air Navigators was set up in 1929, and became a Livery Company only in 1956. The most recently formed of London's eighty-four Companies is the Company of Scientific Instrument Makers, established as a gild in 1955 and granted livery status in 1963. Although many of the old Companies have now lost their close association with their own trades, most have found some useful contribution to make to that trade, or an allied craft. The Leathersellers, for example, established the National Leathersellers' College in Bermondsey, and the Horners' Company now have close links with the plastics industry. A few Companies, notably the Fishmongers and the Goldsmiths, still fulfil their original functions and are responsible for the maintenance of standards within their trades.

The Brewers have also endeavoured to preserve their Company as an active trade body, and have continued to restrict membership only to people involved at a high level in the brewing industry. The potential of the Company as a trade organization was rediscovered by the London brewers at the end of the nineteenth century, at a time when the industry found itself under attack from several quarters. Most active in opposition was the Temperance movement, and it was partly a result of this campaign that successive licensing Acts had placed increasing restrictions on both wholesale and retail trade. And the trade itself was divided, with the tied-house system operated by the big breweries being heavily criticized by small traders who had managed to stay independent.

By the turn of the century Court membership had become the exclusive privilege of directors of the eleven major brewery companies named in the previous chapter, and it became customary for a retiring member to nominate his successor from his own company. All the companies represented agreed to abide by the Court's trade rules governing prices. The smaller firms in the London area had no body to represent them until 1893 when the London Brewers' Association was formed. Composed of representatives from about fifty breweries, including the large Court companies, its aim was to promote the exchange of views and co-operation in countering attacks on the brewing trade. Just as a hundred years before, the Brewers' Company had maintained a close link with the Committee of Porter Brewers, so now it became involved in the new London Brewers' Association, as meetings were held at Brewers' Hall.

The passing of the 1904 Licensing Act, the culmination of several pieces of restrictive legislation, was of major importance in the brewing industry. The Act aimed at implementing some of the recommendations of the 1899 Royal Commission on the Liquor Licensing Laws (the Peel Commission), whose report reflected the increase in drunkenness in society. An earlier Act (1901) had already been aimed at one most serious abuse, by forbidding the sale of any intoxicating liquor to children under fourteen; the 1904 Act extended controls over the retail trade by authorizing licences to publicans for a limited term of seven years; justices were also given the right to attach conditions when granting new licences if this seemed desirable, and if licences were taken away for any reason other than misconduct, the licensee was entitled to compensation, to be found by the trade.

It was after the passing of this Act that the three main 'regional associations' of the brewing trade, the London Brewers' Association, the County Brewers' Society and the Burton Brewers'

The modern Dame Alice Owen's School in Potters Bar, Herts. *Collection Dame Alice Owen's School*

Association, joined forces to establish the Brewers' Society as a national body to represent and formulate policies for the industry as a whole. The birth of the Society acknowledged that the increase in mechanization and the great improvements in transport and communications meant for the first time that it was realistic to consider problems on a national rather than merely regional level. The London Brewers, however, still regarded their own Association as useful in dealing with problems peculiar to London, and the Association continued to meet first as 'Brewers trading in London', and then, re-formed after the First World War, as the London Brewers' Council.

The new Council met, as its predecessor had, at Brewers' Hall; the Company's Assistant Clerk was appointed Secretary, and the Master of the Company was the *ex-officio* Chairman. Membership was confined to brewers trading within the Metropolitan Police area, and the Council's declared object was 'to establish throughout the area a policy of unity of action in all matters of common interest'. The value of the Council's work should not be under-estimated, for in some matters it gave the lead to the trade throughout the country. One important aspect of its work was establishing standard sizes and designs for bottles and tops. Brewers who belonged to the Court were all naturally members of the Council, so the links between the two organizations remained close, and trade matters were more likely to be discussed and resolved by the Council than the Court. The Court, however, continued to have trade rules for its own members, and after 1910 special 'Trade Meetings' of the Court were held for dealing specifically with trade rather than Company business.

The war of 1914–18 had some lasting consequences for the brewing industry throughout the country. The urgent need to control drunkenness resulted in legislation which reduced the opening hours for on and off licences and a strict control was imposed on gravity, and on prices. The war did not, however, seem greatly to have affected the Brewers' Company; the Court continued to meet through the war years and the only major innovation was the decision not to hold the usual annual elections to office. Cecil Lubbock, Master at the outbreak of war, remained in office for the duration. The annual feasts had ended several years before the outbreak of war owing to lack of money, or at least, not so much the lack of it, as the devotion of greater sums to charity, in compliance with the guidelines of the Livery Commission Report. The last Company dinner was held in 1911, but for several years prior to that, dinners had not been held regularly every year. When the question of another dinner was raised at a Court meeting in 1913 it was decided instead to use the money for a substantial donation to the London Hospital. Once Britain had entered the war, there was, of course, no question of further dinners, and even afterwards they were not revived.

The Second World War of 1939–45 had far greater consequences for the Company, for on the night of 29 December

1940, Brewers' Hall, together with several other livery halls in the same area of the City, was destroyed in an enemy air raid. Virtually nothing of the old Stuart hall survived except some small pieces of leaded window-panes which the Company has kept. It was very fortunate that the Company's important records, charters and other valuable items had been placed in the custody of the Guildhall Library, and so were saved from destruction. Other items were saved by having been kept in a fire-proof safe; among these was the Company's Scrapbook, the edges of the pages of which were charred by the intense heat of the fire.

Even after this bombing, however, the Company continued to function, and the Court met as was customary every month, except for August and September, throughout the war years, using offices in the Cannon Brewery. Later they moved to offices in 66 Cheapside, EC2, and in 1945 the Company moved again, to premises in 18 Mansfield Street, W1, until the new hall was completed in July 1960. The decision to rebuild the hall was taken soon after the war; the Court was unanimous in the wish to maintain the centuries of tradition and retain the freehold of the site for a new hall. A Hall Committee was appointed by the Court to supervise the project, which took fifteen years to complete. The Company had to face three lengthy public inquiries before the City granted planning permission. The municipal authorities were keen to purchase the freehold themselves, and draw up their own plans for comprehensive redevelopment of war-damaged areas. While not opposed to any new livery hall, they favoured plans for incorporating Brewers' Hall in a large office block, an idea totally opposed by members of the Company.

It was not until 1958 that permission for the present hall was granted, though the Company had to compromise by surrendering part of their freehold to the City. Sir Hubert Worthington, R.A., was chosen as the architect of the new hall, to be a three-storey building, with the main suite of rooms on the first floor as they had been in the Stuart hall. The exterior, of Portland stone, is somewhat severe, and gives quite a different impression from the elegance and warmth of the oak staircase and the panelled hall and the courtroom with beautiful hand-carved architraves. When the hall was completed the Court held a small

Stanley Spencer's *Crucifixion*, from the chapel at Aldenham School.
Aldenham School

party for the carvers and other craftsmen who had contributed
to the building to show their appreciation of the high standards
of workmanship involved. The livery hall itself, panelled in oak,
has the arms of the Company at one end, above a pediment, and,
opposite, the arms of Charles II, above the door leading to the
court room. Other coats-of-arms displayed above the panelling
are those of the City of London, Thomas à Becket, and the
Company's principal benefactors, Richard Platt, Dame Alice
Owen, Samuel Starling, Samuel Whitbread, James Hickson and
Harry Charrington. The shelves beneath the pediment are used
to display the Company's silver on ceremonial occasions and

The courtyard of Brewers' Hall, Addle Street, completed in 1673

other items of interest are exhibited in two display cases just recently given to the Company. The ground floor of the hall is at present let as offices to the Royal Bank of Canada, and the Company's own offices are on the second floor, with a flat for the Beadle at one end. Every detail of the building, decoration and the procuring of suitable furniture was carefully supervised by the members of the Hall Committee, who gave a great deal of time and energy to ensure that the new hall would be a worthy successor to the two earlier buildings. The Chairman of the Committee himself worked the seat-covers for the committee-

After the blitz, 1940

room chairs, which depict the coats-of-arms of the Company and its benefactors.

Although the hall was not completed until the end of August 1960, the Clerk and the secretarial staff moved into the offices in July, and the first Court meeting in the new hall was also held in July. The hall was not opened officially till November of that year, when it was blessed by the Bishop of London and the Company entertained the Lord Mayor, to mark the occasion. The total cost of the new building was £133,000, most of which was covered by War Damage payments and sale of part of the

Company's freehold to the City. Many items to furnish the hall were given, either by individual Court members or by Companies, and others have followed over the years, replacing some of the treasures lost in the old hall.

The years after the war brought many changes in every field, as the country settled down to peace and industrial reconstruction. In the brewing industry, the war dealt the final blow to most of the small independent brewers, whose days had first been numbered 150 years earlier, with the advent of the industrial revolution and the growth of the big breweries. Many small businesses suffered in the same way; many had been neglected during the war, and now they were no longer economically viable and could not compete with the big firms with capital to invest in expansion. Small breweries were taken over by the big companies; others amalgamated, and the major London companies were soon running businesses with interests far beyond the London region.

As the brewery companies became national rather than regional bodies, the functions of regional organizations changed. The London Brewers' Council as a separate organization became something of an anomaly, as the Brewers' Society dealt with trade affairs at a national level and the Brewers' Company, whose members were drawn from some of the largest national breweries, now represented virtually all London interests. Thus in 1972 the London Brewers' Council was absorbed into the Trade Committee of the Court of the Brewers' Company. This Committee was formed as a result of the Company's own reappraisal of the part it could now play in the nationally orientated trade. The Company had never attempted to spread its influence beyond the London area, but members now had wider interests and so turned increasingly to the Brewers' Society in trade affairs. But after the war the Brewers' Company still continued to have two important trade responsibilities. Wages for brewery workers in the London area were agreed by the Wages Committee, which negotiated directly with the trade unions on behalf of the companies represented on the Court. Also, the 1945 Licensing Planning Act, which, through the licensing justices, exercised control over all licensed premises, resulted in the formation of the Reconstruction and Planning Committee,

Interior of the Stuart hall, 1939

The courtroom, with Samuel Starling's wainscotting

The Master's chair

where member companies could consider applications for new on and off licences in the area and by mutual agreement ensure that every locality should have a reasonable choice of public houses.

The Reconstruction and Planning Committee still continues in this role, but the work of the Wages Committee as a negotiating body was brought to an end when in 1972 the unions gave notice of their intention to end the negotiating agreement and in future to deal directly with individual companies. This meant that the Brewers' Company's active participation in important trade affairs was considerably diminished, but members of the Court were unanimous in wishing to maintain the Company's position as a working trade organization, and this was to continue through the newly formed Trade Committee, established in 1971 to 'watch over and promote the interests of the Brewing Industry in Greater London under the general direction of the Court of the Brewers' Company'. The Wages Committee continues to meet, providing a valuable forum for discussion on topics of regional interest.

The rules of the Trade Committee state that 'every Brewery Company based in the United Kingdom and trading within the boundary of Greater London shall be entitled to representation on the Trade Committee', and also allow for any brewery company trading in the area to apply for representation should they wish. This allows for the widest possible membership covering all trade in the London area, an indication of the Company's wish to keep abreast with modern trade developments. At the time that the Trade Committee was inaugurated the Court also brought the Company's own constitution under review, with the intention of opening membership to some other leading breweries who could not qualify under the rules then in operation. The revised rules adopted by the Court in 1973 extended membership to representatives of 'Eligible Companies', such a company being defined as 'a Brewery Company brewing or having a substantial trading interest within Greater London or such wider area as the Court in its discretion may from time to time determine'.

The most immediate effect of this widening of membership was to allow representatives of the Allied and Guinness breweries to sit on the Court. This was a significant change of policy from that adopted by the Court in the early years of the century, when Guinness's policy of importing their brew and not owning their own retail outlets was much criticized. Earlier this century a resolution was passed by the Court to prohibit the sale of Guinness in any of their members' tied houses!

The new rules also make it possible for the Court to admit a limited number (maximum of six) of personal members (as opposed to representative members who sit as directors of their companies). Personal members are defined as those 'who have rendered exceptional and notable service to, or have close affiliations with, the Brewers' Company or the Brewing Industry'. The practice of electing new members to the freedom, the livery and the Court at one and the same time is still followed, and retiring Court members still retain livery membership. The Court has also occasionally granted honorary membership of the livery to persons who have rendered especial service to the industry and the Company. In recent years the only person to be so honoured has been the then Clerk, who served the Company for many years until his retirement in October 1975.

The admission of personal members to the Court has made it possible for the Company to retain the services of several persons who would otherwise have automatically retired on ceasing to be directors of eligible companies. This has been particularly valuable in the administration of the Company's charities, for several of the present personal members continue to play a very active part in this field, which is of great importance to the Company as its main charities are continuing to thrive. The almshouses at Aldenham and South Mimms are still in use and have been equipped with modern bathrooms, telephone and central heating. Aldenham School expanded considerably in the post-war years and in 1962 a fifth boarding-house, Kennedy's, was completed, so the school can now take up to 360 boys. The new chapel, another post-war addition, now houses a remarkably fine organ and two outstanding Stanley Spencer paintings, the latter being a gift from the present Chairman of the Governors. The Platt endowment is unfortunately not large, but the school's facilities have been improved and modernized in recent years, largely from funds raised by

The oak-panelled livery hall today, with the Company arms above the ceremonial display cabinet

appeals, and also with considerable sums contributed by the Brewers' Company.

The Dame Alice Owen Schools have benefited greatly from the income from the Ermitage Fields estate, and both the boys' and the girls' schools have earned high reputations. The girls' school was destroyed by bombing in October 1940, and the new buildings were only completed in 1963. Under the 1944 Education Act the schools took on voluntary aided status to enable them to continue without charging fees, receiving aid within the state education system, but still retaining a measure of independence. In the last decade, however, it became increasingly clear that the schools had little future in Islington. The site, in the middle of a densely built-up area, offered no possibility for new buildings, and the boys' school premises, most of which dated from the 1880s, were becoming inadequate. Furthermore, the school population in Islington was declining. After much deliberation and negotiation it was decided that the two schools should amalgamate to form a co-educational comprehensive school, and move out of London. After several possible areas were explored, a fine site was acquired at Potters Bar, Hertfordshire, complete with lake and woods. The first pupils arrived in September 1973 at a school which was still largely a building site. The buildings were completed in 1976. New as it is, the school has already earned an excellent reputation in the area, and the buildings were officially opened in June 1976.

The new Owen's School might be regarded as a symbol of how the Brewers' Company has adapted itself to the needs of the twentieth century: an old foundation, still working to fulfil its original aims, but in ways most suited to modern conditions. Just so has the Brewers' Company itself come to terms with contemporary demands, while continuing to work for the promotion of the brewing industry and of the charities for which it is responsible. More changes will undoubtedly come in the future, but the Company will still be guided by these aims, and so well has it succeeded in meeting the challenges of the past 500 years that one cannot doubt its ability to continue to do so. For those whose task it will be to carry on the Company's traditions, its history will, it is hoped, be an encouragement, and so

May the Brewers' Company, root and branch,
In prosperity flourish forever!

Notes, Appendices, Bibliography and Index

Notes

CHAPTER 1

1. R. Sharpe (ed.), *Calendar of Letter Books of the City of London*, Book C, p. 7. These Letter Books are records of the daily business of the Guildhall, and are frequently referred to in the text. The volumes are in chronological order, each known by a letter of the alphabet.
2. From available records it seems that the Weavers were possibly the pioneers of the trade organization, but the evidence is not conclusive.
3. Tacitus, *Germania*, Chapter 23, V.
4. Caesar, *De Bello Gallico*, Bk. I, Chapter 5.
5. Some of the most popular were clerk-ales (in aid of the local clergy) and bride-ales (for betrothed couples).
6. G. Greenaway (ed.), *Life of Thomas à Becket, based on an account by William Fitzstephen*, the Folio Society, 1961, p. 46.
7. *Letter Book A*, p. 216.
8. *Letter Book H*, p. 201.
9. Stow, *Survey of London*, 1603 text, ed. C. L. Kingsford, Oxford 1971, Vol. 1, p. 33.
10. George Unwin, *The Gilds and Companies of London*, Frank Cass, 1963, p. 108.
11. Unwin examines adulterine gilds in some detail.
12. R. Sharpe (ed.), *Calendar of Wills in the Court of Hustings*, Vol. 2, p. 26.
13. Geoffrey Chaucer, *The Canterbury Tales*, Prologue, ll. 747–50.
14. *Letter Book E*, p. 13.

CHAPTER 2

1. *Letter Book D*, p. 248.
2. *Letter Book E*, p. 71.
3. *Letter Book F*, p. 245.
4. *Letter Book H*, p. 167.

5. Ibid., p. 373.

6. Quoted in F. A. King, *Beer Has a History*, 1947. Original source uncertain, though similar incidents are recorded in the Letter Books.

7. *Letter Book A*, p. 220.

8. *The Harrowing of Hell*, Coventry cycle of Mystery Plays, ll. 710–43.

9. *Letter Book D*, p. 237.

10. Ibid., p. 259.

11. *Letter Book F*, p. 107.

12. *Letter Book D*, p. 299.

13. *Letter Book H*, pp. 183–4.

14. *Letter Book G*, p. 76.

15. Ibid., p. 172.

16. *Letter Book H*, p. 43.

17. Ibid., p. 39.

18. W. Herbert, *History of the Twelve Great Livery Companies*, 1836. The list of those returned to the 1376 Council appears in *Letter Book H*, pp. 42–4; Herbert appears to have misread this.

19. *Letter Book H*, Introduction, p. XXIII.

20. Such inter-trade skirmishes continued for many years. In his *Diary* for 1668 Samuel Pepys recorded this 'great discourse of the fray' between butchers and weavers:

At first the butchers knocked down all weavers that had green or blue aprons, till they were fain to pull them off and put them in their breeches. At last the butchers were fain to pull off their sleeves, that they might not be known, and were soundly beaten out of the field, and some deeply wounded and bruised; till at last the weavers went out triumphing, calling £100 for a butcher.

21. *Letter Book H*, p. 336.

CHAPTER 3

1. *Letter Book I*, p. 50.

2. Ibid., p. 51.

3. Ibid., p. 50.

4. Ibid., pp. 97–8.

5. Ibid., pp. 232–3.

6. Ibid., p. 235.

7. Ibid., p. 236.

8. William Porland's Minute Book, p. 1. Porland used Latin, Norman French and English in his records (see Chapter 5). Where necessary, quotations have been translated.

9. Porland, p. 20.

10. Ibid., p. 23.

11. Ibid., p. 32.

12. Ibid., p. 69B.

13. Ibid., p. 50.

14. Ibid., p. 72B.
15. Ibid., p. 120.
16. The Company's charters, together with most of the records prior to 1890, are now kept in the Guildhall Library.
17. Porland, p. 290.
18. Ibid., p. 328.
19. *Letter Book K*, p. 354.

CHAPTER 4

1. Porland, p. 69B.
2. Ibid., p. 15B.
3. Ibid., p. 2.
4. Ibid., p. 11.
5. Ibid., p. 83.
6. Ibid., pp. 93–4.
7. Ibid., pp 98 and 100.
8. Ibid., p. 143.
9. Ibid., p. 17.
10. Ibid., p. 161.
11. Ibid., p. 50.
12. Ibid., p. 157.
13. Ibid., pp. 134–5.
14. Ibid., p. 244.
15. Ibid., pp. 22 and 16.
16. Ibid., p. 46.
17. Ibid., p. 265B.
18. Ibid., p. 26B.
19. Ibid., p. 52B.
20. Ibid., p. 236.
21. Ibid., p. 290.
22. Ibid., p. 56.
23. Ibid., p. 56.
24. Ibid., p. 20.
25. Ibid., p. 71.
26. Ibid., p. 324.

CHAPTER 5

1. *Letter Book L*, p. 211.
2. Petition quoted in King, p. 58.
3. *Letter Book L*, pp. 295–7.
4. Ibid., pp. 52–3.
5. Ibid., p. 157.
6. Ibid., pp. 200–3.

7. Ibid., p. 295.
8. *Letter Book I*, pp. 233–5.
9. Shakespeare, *Henry IV, Part II*, Act 11, Sc. 4, ll. 91–102.
10. Ale-houses had by now adopted the practice of having individual signs hung on their poles; the first modern inn-signs.

CHAPTER 6

1. *Letter Book I*, Introduction, p. XXXII.
2. 'The Great Twelve' Companies are (in order of precedence)

1. Mercers	7. Merchant Taylors
2. Grocers	8. Haberdashers
3. Drapers	9. Salters
4. Fishmongers	10. Ironmongers
5. Goldsmiths	11. Vintners
6. Skinners	12. Clothworkers

3. The pall is at present on long-term loan to the Museum of London.
4. Richard Platt's Letters Patent are still in the Company's possession, in the custody of the Guildhall Library, MS No. 5439.
5. The original orders are fully transcribed in R. J. Evans, *The History of Aldenham School*, Hazell, Watson and Viney, 1969.
6. The original grants of arms are in the Guildhall Library. Two excellent copies are on display at Brewers' Hall.
7. Stow, Vol. 11, p. 451.
8. Unwin, pp. 238–9.
9. Thomas Fuller, 'English Worthies', 1662, quoted in *Life in Shakespeare's England*, ed. John Dover Wilson
10. King, p. 97.

CHAPTER 7

1. Cf. V. Pearl, *London and the Outbreak of the Puritan Revolution*, 1961, p. 299. When in 1669 Samuel Starling, Past Master of the Brewers' Company, became Lord Mayor, he felt obliged to join the Drapers' Company.
2. The full account of the Livery Companies' involvement in Ireland can be found in *A Digest of the Origin, Formation and Proceedings of the Irish Society*, privately printed in 1841 for the Companies concerned. The Brewers' Company sold their Ulster lands between 1892 and 1902.
3. Quoted in J. Bickerdyke, *Curiosities of Ale and Beer*, 1886, p. 146.
4. Ibid., p. 116.
5. The Brewers were not the only Company to be forced to sell valuables; even the wealthy Goldsmiths had to sell much of their plate to rebuild.
6. Cf. Samuel Pepys's *Diary* for 9 September 1666.
7. Brewers' Company Scrapbook, p. 106.

8. Cf. P. Mathias, *The Brewing Industry in England, 1700–1830*, Cambridge, 1959, pp. 220–2. Thrale's brewery was sold after his death in 1791 to Robert Barclay and John Perkins.

9. Porter was also popularly known as 'Entire'.

10. Brewers' Company Scrapbook, p. 204.

11. Ibid., p. 278.

12. Ibid., p. 66.

13. Ibid., p. 562.

14. Ibid., p. 360.

CHAPTER 8

1. Brewers' Company Business Book, 1858–66, p. 2.

2. Brewers' Company Memorandum Book, 1834–88, p. 256.

3. Cf. Item 13 of agenda quoted above.

4. *Livery Commission Report*, 1884.

5. Cf. R. A. Dare, *A History of Owen's School*, Carwal, 1963.

6. Brewers' Company Scrapbook, p. 576.

7. The Company sold its barge in the early nineteenth century. It was used for many years on ceremonial occasions to take the Masters and Wardens and other members of the Company for royal processions on the Thames and also for Lord Mayor's Day. The Company still has the two sixteen-foot long barge banners which flew on the barge, and also the silver bargemaster's badge.

8. Brewers' Company Scrapbook, p. 408.

9. *Livery Commission Report*, 1884.

Clerks to the Brewers' Company

Figures in plain type denote dates of appointment and resignation or death. Figures in italics denote years during which a person is known to have been Clerk, dates of appointment and/or resignation being unknown. Records for the early years are incomplete.

John Morey	? –1418
William Porland	1418–1440
Robert Cokat	1440– ?
John Bowgham	1554– ?
Roger Egliston	*1568–1596*
William Atkinson	*1597–1628*
Mathew Hancock	1628–1655
John Colwell	1655–1667
Thomas Slater	1667–1685
Samuel Gee	1685–1707
Charles Michel	1707–1723
Charles Bernard	1723–1739
William Coward	1739–1757
Alexander Whitchurch	1757–1782
Bury Hutchinson	1782–1824
William Vines	1824–1848
Charles Richard Vines	1848–1880
William Charles Higgins	1880–1920
Colonel Emrys Hunter Evans	1920–1947
Denis Richard Ledward	1947–1955
Brigadier Ronald Gordon, O.B.E.	1955–1960
Richard Charles Stanley-Baker	1960–1975
Melville John Adams	1975–

Masters of the Brewers' Company

It was only during the mid-sixteenth century that it became the practice to elect one Master annually. Gaps have been left in this list where the records for the year in question are either no longer extant or incomplete.

1563	William Beswicke		1591	Robert Allesson
1564	William Beswicke		1592	Thomas Veary
1565	John Dauldron		1593	William Maskall (died)
1566	—			John Newnam
1567	Robert Wood		1594	Mathew Merten
1568	Roger Bellowe		1595	Robert Allesson
1569	Roger Pynder		1596	Syracke Rose
1570	Robert Crippes		1597	John Newnam
1571	Thomas Etheridge		1598	Allen Downer
1572	Thomas Hasilwood		1599	William Stratton
1573	Robert Shawe		1600	—
1574	John Harrisson		1601	Francis Snellinge
1575	Richard Eskridge		1602	Thomas Draper
1576	Richard Platt		1603	—
1577	William Beswicke		1604	Thomas Hadden
1578	William Beswicke		1605	James Eynion
1579	Thomas Hasillwood		1606	Henry Draper
1580	Humfrey Powell		1607	Thomas Scoles
1581	Richard Platt		1608	John Hall (ill)
1582	Richard Eskridge			Henry Draper
1583	Mathew Merten		1609	Roger Bellowe
1584	John Stevens		1610	Francis Snellinge
1585	John Trene		1611	John Yorke
1586	John Braytofte		1612	John Willand
1587	John Hill		1613	Thomas Brickwood
1588	Christopher Butler		1614	Peter Browne
1589	William Freman		1615	Jeffrey Spencer
1590	John Newnam		1616	Thomas Cutts

1617	Thomas Sakry	1661	Alderman and Sheriff
1618	William Harrison		Samuell Starling, formerly
1619	John Watts		Sternell
1620	William Stevens	1662	William Greene
1621	Edward Emmerson	1663	Emery Hill
1622	James Desmeistres	1664	Henry Kettle
1623	George Brookeshawe	1665	James Walker
1624	Thomas Blisse	1666	Thomas Grimshaw
1625	Edmounde Morgan	1667	Alderman Willam Dashwood
1626	Henrie Hodge	1668	Alderman John Foorth
1627	James Desmeistres	1669	—
1628	William Carpenter	1670	Alderman Dannet Foorth
1629	William Hobby	1671	Tristram May
1630	John Heylyn	1672	James Reading
1631	Samuell Cranmer	1673	Richard Lowe
1632	Francis Zachary	1674	John Collins
1633	John Ridgway	1675	John Wilcocks
1634	Richard Rochdale	1676	Henry Sell
1635	James Browne	1677	Ralph Bowes
1636	Bartholomew Parker	1678	James Reading
1637	Robert Draper	1679	Sir Jonathan Raymond,
1638	Alderman Samuel Cranmer		Kt, Sheriff
1639	Henry Leake	1680	John Freeman
1640	Richard Harford	1681	John Freind
1641	John Greate	1682	Joseph Laurence
1642	Edward Buckley	1683	—
1643	John Bide	1684	William Curtis
1644	Joseph Jaques	1685	William Carpenter
1645	John Parsons	1686	William Carpenter
1646	John Gwalter	1687	Captain John Pery
1647	Leonard Hamond	1688	John Raymond
1648	Stephen Sedgwick	1689	Alderman Sir John
1649	Henry Greene		Parsons, Kt
1650	Robert Houghton	1690	Robert Breedon
1651	John James	1691	John Crosse
1652	Robert Jaques	1692	Thomas Ayres
1653	John Box	1693	James Child
1654	John Parsons	1694	John Raymond
1655	Samuel Sternell	1695	Matthew Walraven
1656	William Hiccocks	1696	Abraham Chitty
1657	John Davis	1697	Abraham Chitty
1658	Edward Lawrence (died)	1698	Major William Woodroff
	Samuell Sternell, Snr	1699	Thomas Freeman
1659	Richard Loton	1700	Timothy Lanoy
1660	William Carpenter	1701	John England

1702	Edward Godfrey	1744	Andrew Hope
1703	Anthony Bond	1745	Charles Osborn
1704	—	1746	Alderman Crispe Gascoyne
1705	Thomas Malyn	1747	William Hagger
1706	John Cholmley	1748	John Scott
1707	Benjamin Green	1749	John Raymond
1708	Charles Cox	1750	Shardlow Wightman
1709	John Clark	1751	Samuel Dickinson
1710	George Meggott	1752	Matthew Dove
1711	Charles Feltham	1753	Joseph Foster
1712	Thomas Cole	1754	Henry Willoughby
1713	Thomas Cole	1755	Henry Willoughby
1714	Sir Robert Breedon, Kt, Sheriff	1756	John Stubbs
1715	Edmund Halsey	1757	Daniel Booth
1716	Felix Feast	1758	Peter Greene
1717	Felix Feast	1759	Richard Hare
1718	Samuel Mayo	1760	Nathaniel Scott
1719	Joseph Townsend	1761	William Mason
1720	Joseph Townsend	1762	William Raper
1721	Captain Joseph Bird	1763	Charles Hoyle
1722	Thomas Cole	1764	William Seward
1723	Sir Felix Feast (died) Samuel Mayo	1765	William Seward
1724	Joseph Helby	1766	Joseph Dickinson
1725	Joseph Raymond	1767	Henry Mason
1726	Rivers Dickinson	1768	Thomas Curteis
1727	William Tayleure	1769	John Smith
1728	Joseph Nutt	1770	Samuel Hawley
1729	Andrew Crosse	1771	Samuel Hawley
1730	Alderman Humphrey Parsons, Lord Mayor	1772	Felix Calvert
1731	Henry Johnson	1773	Samuel, Lord Hawley
1732	Henry Johnson	1774	Samuel, Lord Hawley
1733	John Kroger	1775	Andrews Pankeman
1734	John Wightman	1776	William Feast
1735	John Wightman	1777	Peter Hamond
1736	Robert Pycroft	1778	Samuel, Lord Hawley
1737	Starkey Mayo	1779	John Curteis
1738	Starkey Mayo	1780	Edward Bond
1739	Samuel How	1781	Leonard Hammond
1740	William Pearce	1782	John Thornton
1741	Alderman William Calvert	1783	John Baker
1742	William Fuller	1784	Richard Kinnersley
1743	Andrew Hope	1785	John Charrington
		1786	Edward Barnes
		1787	Edward Bond
		1788	Richard Hare

1789	Benjamin Smith	1833	John Donaldson
1790	Joseph Gascoyne	1834	James Goding
1791	Thomas Richardson	1835	Joseph Delafield
1792	Samuel Waring	1836	Robert Pryor
1793	William Truman Read	1837	Robert Hanbury
1794	Samuel Waring	1838	George Matthew Hoare
1795	Samuel Waring	1839	Edmund Sexton Pery Calvert
1796	Samuel Waring		
1797	Gideon Combrune	1840	Arthur Kett Barclay
1798	Oliver Dickinson	1841	Richard Martineau
1799	Richard Walford	1842	Alfred Head
1800	Joseph Hale	1843	William Delafield
1801	Thomas Smith	1844	Frederick Woodbridge
1802	William Whitmore	1845	Charles Allen Young
1803	Joseph Kirkman (died) Joseph Hale	1846	Samuel Charles Whitbread
		1847	Samuel Charles Whitbread
1804	Alderman Harvey Christian Combe	1848	Charles Charrington
		1849	John Lettsom Elliot
1805	James Pulleine	1850	Sir Edward North Buxton, Bt
1806	John Martineau		
1807	Daniel Bell	1851	Henry James Hoare
1808	Robert Calvert	1852	John Manning Needham
1809	Sampson Hanbury	1853	Hedworth David Barclay
1810	Robert Kilby Cox	1854	Edward Charrington
1811	John Beardmore	1855	Robert Hanbury, Jnr
1812	Harry Charrington	1856	Charles Hugh Hoare
1813	Robert Barclay	1857	Charles Addington Hanbury
1814	John Bittleston	1858	Philip Worsley
1815	Joseph Delafield	1859	Charles Buxton, M.P.
1816	George Hale	1860	Charles Buxton, M.P.
1817	Timothy Brown	1861	Algernon Perkins
1818	Charles Calvert	1862	James Watney, Jnr
1819	Henry Perkins	1863	Thomas George Barclay
1820	Nicholas Charrington	1864	John Samuel Tanqueray
1821	Charles Cole	1865	Joseph Bonsor
1822	Joseph Tickell	1866	Norman Watney
1823	John Vickris Taylor	1867	Edward Courage
1824	Thomas Fowell Buxton	1868	Richard Henry Combe
1825	John Forster	1869	William Whitbread
1826	Charles Barclay	1870	Sir Thomas Fowell Buxton, Bt
1827	Frederick Perkins		
1828	Nicholas Charrington	1871	Robert Barclay
1829	Thomas Butts Aveling	1872	Frederick Manning Needham
1830	Michael Bland	1873	Barclay Field
1831	Joseph Martineau	1874	Alfred Henry Bevan
1832	Harvey Combe	1875	Edward North Buxton

1876	Augustus Frederick Perkins	1919	Edwyn Frederick Barclay
1877	Charles Combe	1920	Edwyn Frederick Barclay
1878	Spencer Charrington	1921	Edward John Mann
1879	Frederick Lincoln Bevan	1922	Edward Walter Giffard
1880	James Hiscutt Crossman	1923	Percy George Gates, M.P.
1881	Henry Cosmo Orme Bonsor	1924	John Bradshaw
1882	Richard Worsley	1925	Horace Rowland Hill
1883	John Bagot Scriven	1926	Major Arthur Bonsor
1884	Walter Mortimer Allfrey	1927	Captain Guy Nicholas Charrington
1885	George Alexander Bonsor		
1886	Edgar Lubbock	1928	Charles George Field-Marsham
1887	William Hoare		
1888	Edmund Smith Hanbury	1929	Sydney Oswald Nevile
1889	Spencer Calmeyer Charrington	1930	Cecil Ernest Wells Charrington, M.C.
1890	John Henry Buxton	1931	Horace Legard Grimston
1891	William Musgrave Wroughton	1932	Lieutenant-Colonel Edward North Buxton, M.C.
1892	Alfred Money Wigram	1933	Charles Armstrong
1893	Vernon James Watney	1934	Oliver Vernon Watney
1894	Richard Combe	1935	Jack Garton Durrant
1895	George Crafter Croft	1936	Colonel George Bluett Winch
1896	William Thomas Paulin		
1897	Gerald Buxton	1937	William Henry Whitbread
1898	Robert Milburn	1938	Edwin John Venner
1899	Edward Mann	1939	Commander Redmond Walter McGrath
1900	Charles Hagart Babington		
1901	John Mackenzie Hanbury	1940	Commander Redmond Walter McGrath
1902	Charles James Phillips		
1903	Oswald Pearce Serocold	1941	Commander Redmond Walter McGrath
1904	Claude Watney		
1905	Hubert Frederick Barclay	1942	Commander Redmond Walter McGrath
1906	Granville Bevan		
1907	Francis Pelham Whitbread	1943	Commander Redmond Walter McGrath
1908	Malcolm Cosmo Bonsor		
1909	Douglas Crossman	1944	Commander Redmond Walter McGrath
1910	Colonel Francis Charrington C.M.G.	1945	Commander Redmond Walter McGrath
1911	Andrew Richard Motion	1946	John Fowell Buxton
1912	Henry Fowell Buxton	1947	Edward Randal Chadwyck-Healey, M.C.
1913	Cecil Lubbock		
1914	Cecil Lubbock	1948	Frederick Hugh Bowyer, M.B.E.
1915	Cecil Lubbock		
1916	Cecil Lubbock	1949	Maurice Vandeleur Courage
1917	Cecil Lubbock	1950	Douglas Peter Crossman, T.D.
1918	Cecil Lubbock		

1951 Lieutenant-Colonel John Hubert Courage
1952 John Arthur Pepys Charrington
1953 Walter Pearce Serocold, D.S.O., T.D.
1954 Simon Harvey Combe, M.C.
1955 John Edmund Martineau
1956 Peter Pryor
1957 Lieutenant-Colonel William Henry Kingsmill, D.S.O., M.C.
1958 Alan Lewis Wigan
1959 Thomas Brian Bunting
1960 Francis George Mann, D.S.O., M.C.
1961 Sanders Watney
1962 Maurice Arthur Pryor
1963 Frederick Onslow Alexander Godwyn Bennett

1964 Michael George Thomas Webster
1965 Edward Raymond Courage, C.B.E.
1966 Alan Michael Tritton, D.S.C.
1967 Archibald Graham Neale, T.D.
1968 Captain Mason Hogarth Scott, R.N. (Ret'd)
1969 Richard Hubert Courage
1970 Major Alistair Giles Mann
1971 Roger Derek Wise
1972 Edward Hamilton Fleetwood Fuller
1973 Robert Harold Soames
1974 Sir Gerald Bowers Thorley, T.D.
1975 Christopher John Mytton Downes
1976 Major Lewis John Turner, T.D.

Bibliography

ASH, B., *The Golden City; London between the Fires, 1666–1941,* Phoenix House, 1964

BAKER, T., *Medieval London,* Chambers, 1970

BICKERDYKE, J., *Curiosities of Ale and Beer,* Field and Tuer, 1886

BLACKHAM, R. J., *The Soul of the City: London's Livery Companies,* Sampson Low, 1931

DARE, R. A., *A History of Owen's School,* Carwal, 1963

DITCHFIELD, P. H., *The Story of the City Companies,* Foulis & Co, 1926

EVANS, R. J., *The History and Register of Aldenham School,* 10th edition, Hazell, Watson and Viney, 1969

FRENCH, R. V., *Nineteen Centuries of Drink in England,* Longmans, 1884

GEORGE, M. D., *London Life in the Eighteenth Century,* Penguin, 1925

HAZLITT, W. C., *The Livery Companies of the City of London,* Shonnenschein, 1892

HERBERT, W., *History of the Twelve Great Livery Companies,* London, 1836

HOLMES, M. J. R., *Elizabethan London,* Cassell, 1969

KAHL, W. F., *The Development of the London Livery Companies,* Harvard Graduate School of Business Administration, 1960

KING, F. A., *Beer Has a History,* Hutchinson, 1947

KRAMER, S., *The English Craft Gilds,* Columbia University Press, 1927

MATHIAS, P., *The Brewing Industry in England, 1700–1830,* Cambridge University Press, 1959

MONCKTON, H. A., *The English Public House,* Bodley Head, 1969

PEARL, V., *London and the Outbreak of the Puritan Revolution,* Oxford University Press, 1961

REDDAWAY, T. F., *The Rebuilding of London after the Great Fire,* Edward Arnold, 1951

SAMUELSON, J., *History of Drink,* Trübner, 1878

SHARPE, R. R. (ed), *Calendar of Letter Books of the City of London,* London, 1898–1912

SHARPE, R. R. (ed), *Calendar of Wills in the Court of Hustings,* London, 1889–90

SHARPE, R. R., *London and the Kingdom* (3 vols), London, 1894

UNWIN, George, *The Gilds and Companies of London,* Frank Cass, 1963

Index

Note: *Italic figures* refer to illustrations on the pages cited. Names listed on pages 124–30 are not included in index, nor is the Bibliography.